WILD ABOUT
ANIMALS

WILD ABOUT
ANIMALS

WRITTEN BY
JINNY JOHNSON, ANN KAY, STEVE PARKER

Miles
KeLLy

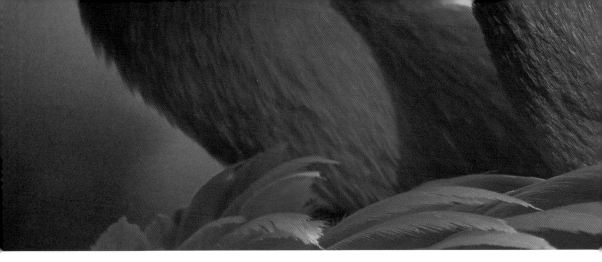

First published in 2017 by Miles Kelly Publishing Ltd
Harding's Barn, Bardfield End Green, Thaxted, Essex, CM6 3PX, UK

This edition printed 2021

2 4 6 8 10 9 7 5 3

Publishing Director Belinda Gallagher
Creative Director Jo Cowan
Editorial Director Rosie Neave
Senior Editors Fran Bromage, Amy Johnson
Editorial Assistant Meghan Oosterhuis
Cover Designer Joe Jones
Designers Rob Hale, Joe Jones, Andrea Slane
Image Manager Liberty Newton
Indexer Jane Parker
Production Controller Jennifer Brunwin
Reprographics Stephan Davis
Assets Lorraine King

Consultants Camilla de la Bédoyère, Steve Parker

ISBN 978-1-78989-159-1

Printed in China

British Library Cataloguing-in-Publication Data
A catalogue record for this book is available from the British Library

Made with paper from a sustainable forest

www.mileskelly.net

Contents

MAMMALS 6

Mammal groups 8
Big and small 10
Speed machines 12
Swimmers and divers 14
Fliers and gliders 16
Life in snow and ice 18
Creatures of the night 20
Family life 22
Desert dwellers 24
On the prowl 26
Fighting back 28
Deep in the jungle 30
Strange foods 32
City creatures 34
Freshwater mammals 36
Plant-eaters 38
Digging deep 40
Mothers and babies 42

BIRDS 44

The bird world 46
Big to tiny 48
Fast movers 50
Superb swimmers 52
Looking good 54
Night birds 56
Home sweet home 58

Great travellers 60
Desert birds 62
Staying safe 64
Amazing eggs 66
Hunters and scavengers 68
Caring for the young 70
Birds of the jungle 72
Flightless birds 74
On the river 76
Finding food 78
Winter birds 80
Special beaks 82

REPTILES AND AMPHIBIANS 84

Scales and slime 86
Sun worshippers 88
Cooler customers 90
Water babies 92
Land babies 94
Little and large 96
Adaptable animals 98
Natural show-offs 100
Sensitive creatures 102
Feeling hungry 104
Fliers and leapers 106
Slitherers and crawlers 108
Fast and slow 110
Champion swimmers 112

Nature's tanks 114
Dangerous enemies 116
Clever mimics 118
Escape artists 120
Mega reptiles 122
Reptiles in danger 124

ENDANGERED ANIMALS 126

Too late to save 128
How we know 130
How endangered? 132
On the critical list 134
All kinds under threat 136
The greatest threat 138
Too many people 140
Pollution problems 142
A change in the weather 144
Poaching and souvenirs 146
Island problems 148
Stop the slaughter 150
A place to live 152
Captive breeding 154
Future help 156

INDEX 158
ACKNOWLEDGEMENTS 160

MAMMALS

1 Mammals are warm-blooded animals with a bony skeleton and fur or hair. Being warm-blooded means that a mammal keeps its body at a constant temperature, even if the weather is very cold. The skeleton supports the body and protects the delicate parts inside, such as the heart, lungs and brain. There is one sort of mammal you know very well, it's you!

▼▶ Two western lowland gorillas meet face to face. Gorillas are highly intelligent mammals and close cousins of humans.

Mammal groups

2 **There are nearly 5500 different types of mammal.** Most mammals have babies that grow inside the mother's body. While a baby mammal grows, a special organ called a placenta supplies it with food and oxygen from the mother's body. These mammals are called placental mammals.

Placenta

Birth canal

▲ A baby elephant in the womb receives nourishment through the placenta.

3 **Not all mammals' young develop inside the mother's body.** Two smaller groups of mammals do things differently. Monotremes, such as platypuses and echidnas (spiny anteaters), lay eggs. The platypus lays her eggs in a burrow, but the echidna keeps her single egg in a special pouch in her belly until it is ready to hatch.

▶ The echidna keeps her egg in a pouch until it hatches after about ten days.

Monotremes

4 **Mammal mothers feed their babies on milk from their own bodies.** The baby sucks this milk from teats on special mammary glands, also called udders or breasts, on the mother's body. The milk contains all the food the young animal needs to help it grow.

8

5 Marsupials give birth to tiny young that finish developing in a pouch. A baby kangaroo is only 2 centimetres long when it is born. Tiny, blind and hairless, it makes its own way to the safety of its mother's pouch. Once there, it latches onto a teat in the pouch and begins to feed.

A joey starts life as a tiny undeveloped baby

Marsupials

▲ A baby kangaroo is called a joey. It stays in the pouch for about six months while it grows.

▼ This reindeer uses its eyes, ears and especially nose to sense the world.

6 Most mammals have good senses of sight, smell and hearing. Their senses help them watch out for enemies, find food and keep in touch with each other. For many mammals, smell is their most important sense. Plant-eaters such as rabbits and deer sniff the air to pick up scents of danger, especially those of predators.

I DON'T BELIEVE IT!
Lemmings are very fast breeders. Females can become pregnant at only 14 days old, and they can produce litters of as many as 12 young every month.

Big and small

7 **The blue whale is the biggest mammal, and one of the largest animals ever known to have lived.** It can measure as long as seven family cars parked end to end, and spends all of its life in the ocean.

8 **The elephant is the biggest land mammal.** There are three kinds of elephant – the African savannah elephant, the African forest elephant, and the Asian elephant. The African savannah elephant is the biggest – a full-grown male may weigh as much as 10 tonnes – more than 100 adult people.

GORILLA
1.75 metres tall

▼ A full-grown male gorilla weighs up to 275 kilograms.

GIRAFFE
5.5 metres tall

▼ The giraffe's height helps it reach juicy leaves at the tops of trees.

9 Gorillas are the biggest primates. Primates are the group of mammals to which chimpanzees and humans belong.

10 The giraffe is the tallest animal, as well as mammal. A male is as tall as three or four people standing on each other's shoulders. Giraffes live in Africa, south of the Sahara desert.

11 The capybara is the largest rodent. It lives around ponds, lakes and rivers in South America. Rodents are the group of mammals that include rats and mice.

CAPYBARA
1.3 metres long

▲ A well-fed capybara weighs over 70 kilograms.

MOUSE DEER
85 centimetres long

▲ The mouse deer is just 30 centimetres in height.

13 The smallest mammal is the tiny hog-nosed bat. A full-grown adult weighs less than a teaspoon of rice!

12 The tiny mouse deer is the size of a hare. Also known as the chevrotain, it lives in African forests.

HOG-NOSED BAT
3 centimetres long

▶ The tiny hog-nosed bat is just 2 grams in weight.

Speed machines

14 **The cheetah can run faster than any other animal.** It can move at about 100 kilometres an hour, but it cannot run this fast for long. The cheetah uses its speed to catch other animals to eat. It creeps towards its prey until it is only about 100 metres away. Then it races towards it at top speed, ready for the final attack.

15 **The pronghorn is slower than the cheetah, but can run for longer.** It can keep up a speed of 70 kilometres an hour for about ten minutes.

▶ The cheetah's long, slender legs and muscular body help it to run fast. The long tail balances the body while it is running.

16 **Even the brown hare can run at more than 70 kilometres an hour.** Its powerful back legs help it move fast enough to escape enemies such as foxes.

◀ For each stride, the brown hare kicks hard backwards with its long rear legs.

SPEED DEMONS!

Ask an adult to measure how far in metres you can run in 10 seconds. Multiply this by 6, and then times the answer by 60 to find out how many metres you can run in an hour. If you divide this by 1000 you will get your speed in kilometres per hour. You will find it will be far less than the cheetah's 100 kilometres an hour!

◀ The red kangaroo can leap 9 or 10 metres in a single bound.

17 The red kangaroo is a champion jumper. It can leap along at 40 kilometres an hour or more. The kangaroo needs to be able to travel fast. It lives in the dry desert lands of Australia and often has to journey long distances to find grass to eat and water to drink.

Swimmers and divers

18 Most swimming mammals have flippers and fins instead of legs. Their bodies have become sleek and streamlined to help them move through the water easily. Seals and sea lions have large, paddle-like flippers that they can use to drag themselves along on land, as well as for swimming power in water. Whales never come to land. They swim by moving their tails up and down and using their front flippers to steer.

▲ The humpback has the largest flippers of any whale, at 5 metres long.

QUIZ

1. How deep can a Weddell seal dive?
2. What is the layer of fat on a seal's body called?
3. How fast can a killer whale swim?

Answers:
1. 750 metres or more
2. Blubber 3. 55 kilometres an hour

19 **The killer whale can reach a speed of 55 kilometres an hour.** A fierce hunter, it uses its speed to chase fast-swimming prey such as squid, fish and seals. It sometimes hunts in groups and will even attack whales. Killer whales live in all the world's oceans. Despite their name, they are the largest member of the dolphin family. They grow up to 10 metres long and weigh as much as 9 tonnes.

◀ Killer whales often leap clear of the water, an action known as breaching.

▼ A mother and baby Weddell seal. The Weddell is a big seal – 3.5 metres long and half a tonne in weight.

20 **The Weddell seal can dive deeper than any other seal.** It goes down to depths of 750 metres or more in its search for cod and other fish. This seal can stay underwater for a long while, and dives of more than an hour have been timed. It lives in the icy waters of Antarctica, and its body is covered with a thick layer of fatty blubber that helps to keep it warm.

Fliers and gliders

21 Bats are the only true flying mammals. They zoom through the air on wings made of skin. These are attached to the sides of their body and supported by specially adapted, extra-long bones of the arms, hands and fingers. Bats generally hunt at night. During the day they hang upside down by their feet from a branch or cave ledge. Their wings are neatly folded at their sides or around their body.

Finger bones

▶ At dusk, bats leave their resting place, or roost, to feed.

Forearm bone

Finger claw

Wing membrane of skin and thin muscle

◀ Powerful muscles in the bat's chest flap its wings up and down.

22 There are more than 1200 types of bat. They live in most parts of the world, but not in colder areas. Bats feed on many different sorts of food. Most common are the insect-eating bats, which snatch their prey from the air while in flight. Others feast on pollen and nectar from flowers. Flesh-eating bats catch fish, birds, lizards and frogs.

23 Flying lemurs don't really fly – they just glide from tree to tree. They can glide distances of up to 100 metres with the help of flaps of skin at the sides of the body. When the flying lemur takes off from a branch it holds its limbs out, stretching the skin flaps so that they act like a parachute.

▼ The skin flaps of the flying lemur, or colugo, are not only along the sides, but also between the rear legs and tail.

I DON'T BELIEVE IT!

The vampire bat is a blood-drinker! It consumes about 26 litres of blood a year – about the total blood supply of five human beings!

24 Other gliding mammals are flying squirrels and gliders. All can glide from tree to tree, like the flying lemur, with the help of flaps of skin at the sides of the body. Flying squirrels live in North America and parts of Asia. Gliders are a type of possum and live in Australia and New Guinea.

Life in snow and ice

25 The polar bear is the biggest land predator. This Arctic hunter can run fast, swim well and even dive under the ice to hunt its main prey – seals. It also catches seabirds and land animals such as the Arctic hare and reindeer.

▶ The polar bear's thick, white fur helps to keep it warm – even the soles of its feet are furry.

26 Caribou, also known as reindeer, feed in Arctic lands. The land around the Arctic Ocean is called the tundra. In the short summer, plenty of plants grow, the caribou eat their fill and give birth to their young. When summer is over, the caribou trek up to 1000 kilometres south to spend the winter in forests.

27 Some Arctic animals such as the Arctic hare and the ermine, or stoat, change colour. In winter these animals have white fur, which helps them hide among the snow. In summer, when white fur would make them very easy to spot, their coats turn brown.

◀ Reindeer scrape and nose into snow to find plants to eat.

28 The Arctic ground squirrel digs its own burrow system to shelter in, or renovates an old, unoccupied set of burrows. It lines the main nest area with dry grass, moss and thin stems. Here it hibernates for half the year or more – from August to the following April.

29 The leopard seal is one of the fiercest hunters in the Antarctic. It lives in the waters around Antarctica and preys on penguins, fish and other seals. There are no land mammals in the Antarctic.

▲ After waking from hibernation, plants, seeds and berries make up the diet of the Arctic ground squirrel.

30 The walrus has tusks that grow as long as one metre. It uses them to drag itself out of water and onto the ice as well as for defence against enemies and for display against rival walruses.

31 The musk ox has a long shaggy outer coat to help it survive the Arctic cold. A thick undercoat keeps out the damp. The musk ox eats grass, moss and lichen. In winter it digs through the snow with its hooves to reach its food.

▼ Huge male musk ox head–butt to control the herd.

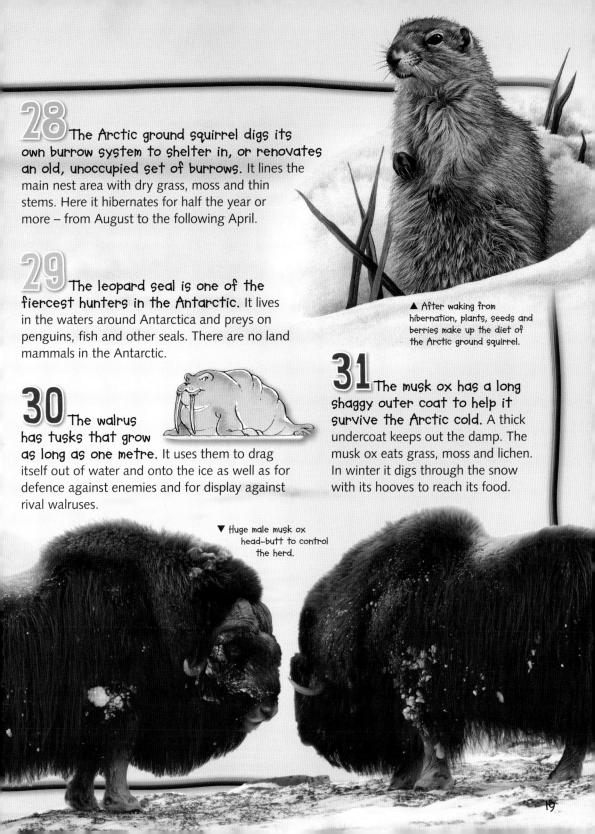

Creatures of the night

32 Not all mammals are active during the day. Some sleep during daylight and wake up at night. They are nocturnal, and there are many reasons for their habits. Overall there are fewer predators active at night, and it is easier to hide in gloomy undergrowth and dark corners.

33 The aye-aye is a strange tree-dwelling lemur of Madagascar. Like many nocturnal animals it has large eyes to collect as much light as possible. It sleeps by day in a nest of leaves and twigs and searches at night for grubs and other small creatures, using its very long fourth finger to pull them from under bark.

▲ An aye-aye probes into holes in trunks and branches for food.

QUIZ

1. What word describes animals that are active at night?
2. Where does the aye-aye live?
3. What does the red panda eat?

Answers:
1. Nocturnal 2. Madagascar
3. Bamboo shoots, fruit, acorns, insects, birds' eggs

34 The red panda is a night feeder. It sleeps during the day, but at night it searches for food such as bamboo shoots, roots, fruit and acorns. It also eats insects, birds' eggs and small animals. In summer, red pandas sometimes wake in the day to climb trees to find fresh leaves to eat.

35 Hyenas usually come out at night to find food. They hunt their own prey and are also scavengers – they feed on the remains of creatures killed by larger hunters. When a lion has eaten its fill, hyenas rush in to grab the remains.

36 Bats hunt at night. Insect feeders, such as the horseshoe bat, manage to find their prey by means of a special kind of animal sonar. The bat makes high-pitched squeaks as it flies. If the sound waves from these noises hit an animal, such as a moth, echoes bounce back to the bat. These echoes tell the bat where its prey is.

◄ Hyenas hunt at night using their excellent sense of smell.

Family life

37 Many mammals live alone, except when they have young, but others live in groups. Wolves live in family groups called packs. The pack is led by an adult female and her mate and may include up to 20 animals.

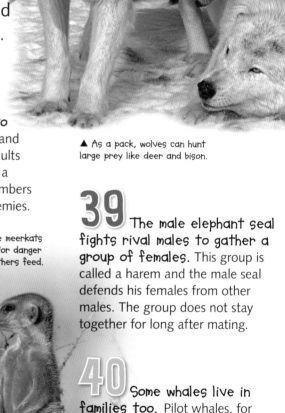

▲ As a pack, wolves can hunt large prey like deer and bison.

38 A type of mongoose called a meerkat lives in large groups of up to 30 animals. The group is called a colony and contains several family units of a pair of adults along with their young. The colony lives in a network of underground burrows. The members of the colony guard each other against enemies.

▼ Some meerkats watch for danger while others feed.

39 The male elephant seal fights rival males to gather a group of females. This group is called a harem and the male seal defends his females from other males. The group does not stay together for long after mating.

40 Some whales live in families too. Pilot whales, for example, live in groups of 20 or more animals that swim and hunt together. A group may include several adult males and a number of females and their young.

41 **Naked mole rats live underground in a colony of animals led by one female.** The colony includes about 100 animals and the ruling female, or queen, is the only one that produces young. Other colony members dig burrows to find food for the group, and look after the queen.

42 **Lions live in groups called prides.** The pride may include one or more adult males, females related to each other, and their young. The average number in a pride is 15. Female young generally stay with the pride of their birth but males must leave before they are full-grown. Lions are unusual in their family lifestyle – most other big cats live alone.

▼ Bonobos are generally peaceful, sharing food with each other.

43 **Bonobos (pygmy chimpanzees) live in large groups, known as communities, of 80 or more.** These are usually a mix of females, males and young. Within the community certain individuals are close friends and interact more than with others. These groups spend time together looking for food, grooming each other, and resting. Sometimes, the whole community gathers to travel, usually led by one or a few females, or to sleep.

25

Desert dwellers

44 Many desert animals burrow underground to escape the scorching heat. The North African gerbil stays hidden all day and comes out at night to eat seeds and insects. This gerbil is so well adapted to desert life that it never needs to drink.

▶ The North African gerbil gets all the liquid it needs from its food.

45 The large ears of the fennec fox help it to lose heat from its body. This fox lives in the North African desert. For its size, it has the largest ears of any dog or fox.

46 Pallas's cat lives in the Gobi Desert. It has thick, long fur to keep it warm in the cold Gobi winter. Pallas's cat lives alone, usually in a cave or a burrow, and hunts mice and birds.

▶ The fennec's huge ears can hear prey as tiny as ants.

47 A camel can last for weeks without drinking. It can manage on the liquid it gets from feeding on desert plants. But when it does find some water it drinks as much as 100 litres at one time. It does not store water in its hump, but it can store fat.

QUIZ

1. How much water can a camel drink in one go?
2. Where does the bactrian camel live?
3. Which animals don't drink?

Answers:
1. 100 litres 2. Gobi Desert
3. North African gerbil and the
kangaroo rat

48 A kangaroo rat never needs to drink. The kidneys control how much water there is in an animal's body. The kangaroo rat's kidneys are much more efficient than ours. It can even make some of its food into water inside its body!

49 The bactrian camel has thick fur to keep it warm in winter. It lives in the Gobi Desert in Asia where winter weather can be very cold indeed. In summer, the camel's long shaggy fur drops off, leaving the camel almost hairless.

50 The desert hedgehog eats scorpions! It carefully nips off the scorpion's deadly sting before eating. It also eats insects and birds' eggs.

◄ The camel's hump fat is broken down into energy and water.

Backbone

Fat in hump

Blood supply

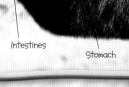

Intestines

Stomach

25

On the prowl

51 Mammals that hunt and kill other creatures to eat are called carnivores. Examples of carnivores are lions, tigers, wolves and dogs. Meat is a more concentrated food than plants so many carnivores do not have to hunt every day. One kill lasts them for several days.

▶ Most carnivores will hunt creatures smaller than themselves. The lion can more easily catch and kill smaller prey like this zebra foal.

52 The tiger is the biggest cat and an expert hunter. It hunts alone, usually for buffalo, deer and wild pigs. The tiger prefers to creep up on prey without being noticed, rather than chase it. Its stripy coat helps it to hide in long grass. When it is as close as possible, the tiger pounces, clamps its jaws around its victim's throat and suffocates it.

▲ A tiger silently stalks its prey, keeping its body low to the ground to remain unseen and unheard.

FOOD CHAIN

Make your own food chain. Draw a picture of a large carnivore such as a lion and tie it to a piece of string. Then draw a picture of an animal that the lion eats such as a zebra. Hang that from the picture of the lion. Lastly draw a picture of lots of grass and plants (the food of the zebra). Hang that from the picture of the zebra.

53 Bears eat many different foods. They are carnivores but most, except for the polar bear, eat more plant material than meat. Brown bears eat fruit, nuts and insects and even catch fish. In summer, when salmon swim up rivers to lay their eggs, the bears wade into the shallows and hook fish with their huge paws.

54 Hunting dogs hunt in packs. Together, they can bring down a much larger animal. The pack sets off after a herd of plant-eaters such as zebras or gazelles. They try to separate one animal that is perhaps weaker or slower from the rest of the herd.

◀ This young wildebeest has been separated from its herd by a pack of African hunting dogs.

Fighting back

▼ Its legs and belly are unprotected, but if attacked the armadillo rolls into a tight ball.

Head and tail fit together to make an armoured 'ball'

55 Some mammals have special ways of defending themselves from enemies. The nine-banded armadillo has body armour. Bony plates, topped with a layer of horn, cover the armadillo's back, sides and head.

56 The porcupine's body is covered with as many as 30,000 sharp spines. When an enemy approaches, the porcupine first rattles its spines as a warning. If this fails, the porcupine runs towards the attacker and drives the sharp spines into its flesh.

Danger past, the armadillo begins to unfurl

◄ The skunk's black-and-white-pattern is a warning that it can spray a horrible fluid.

The armadillo walks away

57 The skunk defends itself with a bad-smelling fluid. This fluid comes from special glands near the animal's tail. If threatened, the skunk lifts its tail and sprays its enemy. The fluid's strong smell irritates the victim's eyes and makes it hard to breathe, and the skunk runs away.

I DON'T BELIEVE IT!

Skunks sometimes feed on bees. They roll the bees on the ground to remove their stings before eating them.

58 A rhinoceros may charge at its enemies at top speed. Rhinos are generally peaceful animals but a female will defend her calf fiercely. If the calf is threatened, she will gallop towards the enemy with her head down and lunge with her sharp horns. Few predators will stay around to challenge an angry rhino.

◀ The sight of a full-grown rhinoceros charging is enough to make most predators turn and run.

59 The pangolin's body is protected by tough overlapping scales. These make the animal look like a giant pine cone. The pangolin feeds mainly on ants and termites and its thick scales protect it from the stinging bites of its tiny prey.

◀ Even the pangolin's long, prehensile (grasping) tail is well protected.

Deep in the jungle

60 Jungle mammals live at all levels of the forest from the tallest trees to the forest floor. Bats fly over the tree tops and monkeys and apes swing from branch to branch. Lower down, smaller creatures, such as civets and pottos, hide in the dense greenery.

▼ The Amazon rainforest echoes at dawn and dusk with howler monkey whoops and screeches.

61 The howler monkey has the loudest voice in the jungle. Each troop of howler monkeys has its own special area, called a territory. Males in rival troops shout at each other to defend their territory. Their shouts can be heard from nearly 5 kilometres away.

▼ Unlike most cats, jaguars like water, where they hunt for fish, turtles and snakes.

62 The jaguar is one of the fiercest hunters in the jungle. It lives in the South American rainforest and is the largest cat in South America. The pig-like peccary and the capybara – a large jungle rodent – are among its favourite prey.

65 Some monkeys have a long tail that they use as an extra limb when climbing. This is called a prehensile tail. It contains a powerful system of bones and muscles so it can be used for gripping.

◄ Sloths live in Central and South American rainforests and swamps – they are surprisingly good swimmers.

63 The sloth hardly ever comes down to the ground. This jungle creature lives hanging from a branch by its special hook-like claws. It is so well adapted to this life that its fur grows downwards – the opposite way to that of most mammals – so that rainwater drips off more easily.

64 Tapirs are pig-like animals that live on the jungle floor. There are three different kinds of tapir in the South American rainforests and one kind in the rainforests of Southeast Asia. Tapirs have long, bendy snouts and they feed on leaves, buds and grass.

◄ The Brazilian tapir is often found near water and is a good swimmer.

66 The okapi uses its long tongue to pick leaves from forest trees. This tongue is so long that the okapi can even lick its own eyes clean!

► Okapis feed in dense, remote rainforests in Central Africa.

Strange foods

67 **Some mammals only eat one or two kinds of food.** The giant panda feeds mainly on the shoots and roots of the bamboo plant. It spends up to 12 hours a day eating, and consumes about 12 kilograms of bamboo a day. The panda also eats small amounts of other plants and sometimes hunts mice and fish.

▶ Giant pandas live in the bamboo forests of central China. There are very few pandas left in the wild, perhaps between 1500 and 3000.

▼ The vampire bat feeds for about 30 minutes, and probably drinks about 26 litres of blood a year.

68 **The vampire bat feeds on blood – it is the only bat that has this special diet.** This bat hunts at night. It finds a victim such as a horse or cow and crawls up its leg onto its body. The bat shaves away a small area of flesh and, using its long tongue, laps up blood that flows from the wound.

69 The mighty blue whale eats only tiny shrimp-like creatures called krill. The whale strains these from the water through a special filter system in its mouth called baleen. It may eat up to 4 tonnes of krill a day.

Krill

▶ Among whales, bowheads have the longest baleen (brush-like strips on the upper jaw), at more than 3 metres.

70 The koala eats the leaves of eucalyptus plants. These leaves are very tough and can be poisonous to many other animals. They do not contain much goodness and the koala has to eat for several hours every day to get enough food. It spends the rest of its time sleeping to save energy. The koala's digestive system has adapted to help it cope with this unusual diet.

71 Tiny ants and termites are the main foods of the giant anteater. The anteater breaks open the insects' nests with its strong, hooked claws. It laps up adult insects plus eggs and young with its sticky 60-centimetre-long tongue.

▶ A giant anteater can consume more than 20,000 ants and termites each day.

City creatures

72 Foxes are among the few larger mammals that manage to survive in towns and cities. They used to find their food in the countryside, but now more and more have discovered that city rubbish bins are a good hunting ground. The red fox will eat almost anything. It kills birds, rabbits, eats insects, fruit and berries and takes human leftovers.

73 Rats will eat almost anything. They have been known to chew through electrical wires, lead piping and even concrete dams. In the US, rats may cause up to one billion dollars' worth of damage every year!

◄ The red fox has spread to all continents except South America and Antarctica, following humans as they throw away food refuse.

▼ The house mouse hides under floors and in cupboards. It will eat any human food it can find, as well as paper, glue and even soap!

74 Rats and mice are among the most successful of all mammals. They live all over the world and eat almost any kind of food. The brown rat and the house mouse are among the most common. The brown rat eats seeds, fruit and grain, but it will also attack birds and mice. In cities it lives in cellars and sewers – anywhere there is rotting food and rubbish.

▼ Young raccoons quickly learn to tip over rubbish bins and tear open plastic bags to get at meal leftovers.

75 Raccoons also live in city areas and raid rubbish bins for food. Like foxes, they eat lots of different kinds of food, including fish, nuts, seeds, berries and insects, as well as what they scavenge from humans. They are usually active at night and spend the day in a den made in a burrow, a hole in rocks or even in the corner of an empty city building.

Freshwater mammals

76 **Most river mammals spend only part of their time in water.** Creatures such as the river otter and the water rat live on land and go into the water to find food. The hippopotamus, on the other hand, spends most of its day in water to keep cool. Its skin needs to stay moist, and it cracks if it gets too dry.

77 **At night hippos leave their river or lake to chomp on land plants.** However they rarely stray far and gallop back to water if danger threatens.

78 **The water vole makes its home in a bankside burrow.** It eats plants growing near the water and in the shallows, and is an expert swimmer.

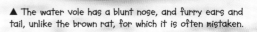
▲ The water vole has a blunt nose, and furry ears and tail, unlike the brown rat, for which it is often mistaken.

79 The platypus uses its duck-like beak to find food on the riverbed. This strange beak is extremely sensitive to touch and to tiny electric currents given off by prey. The platypus dives down to the bottom of the river and digs in the mud for creatures such as worms and shrimps.

◀ When a platypus has found its food, it stores it in its cheeks until it has time to eat it.

80 The otter's ears close off when it is swimming. This stops water getting into them when the otter dives. Other special features are webbed feet, and short, thick fur, which keeps the otter's skin dry.

81 Most dolphins are sea creatures but some live in rivers. There are four different kinds of river dolphins living in rivers in Asia and South America. The baiji of China is now considered to be extinct. All feed on fish and shellfish. They probably use echolocation, a kind of sonar like that used by bats, to find their prey.

▼ The hippo is not a good swimmer but it can walk on the riverbed. It can stay underwater for up to half an hour.

Plant-eaters

82 **In order to get enough nourishment, plant-eaters must spend much of their time eating.** A zebra spends at least half its day munching grass. The advantage of being a plant-eater, though, is that the animal does not have to chase and compete for its food like hunters do.

▼ The Mexican long-tongued bat flaps its wings fast to hover in front of flowers as it feeds.

83 **Some kinds of bat feed on pollen and nectar.** The Queensland blossom bat, for example, has a long brush-like tongue that it plunges deep into flowers to gather its food. As it feeds it pollinates the flowers – it takes the male pollen to the female parts of a flower so that it can bear seeds and fruits.

▼ Carnivores, such as lions, feed on plant-eaters, such as zebras. So there must always be more plant-eaters than carnivores for this 'food chain' to work successfully.

84 **Plants are the main foods of most monkeys.** Monkeys live in tropical forests where there are plenty of fresh leaves and ripe fruit all year round. Some also eat insects and other small creatures.

◄ Seeds and fruit are the main foods of the red uakari, which lives in South American rainforests.

85 **Rabbits have strong teeth for eating leaves and bark.** The large front teeth are called incisors and are used for biting leaves and twigs. The incisors keep growing throughout the rabbit's life – if they did not they would wear out. Rabbits also have broad teeth for chewing.

86 **The manatee is a water-living mammal that feeds on plants.** There are three different kinds of these large, gentle creatures: two live in fresh water in West Africa and in the South American rainforest, and the third lives in the west Atlantic, from Florida to the Amazon.

► Manatees, and their relations dugongs, feed on plants such as water weeds, water lilies and seaweeds.

I DON'T BELIEVE IT!

Manatees are said to have been the origin of sailors' stories about mermaids. Short-sighted sailors may have mistaken these plump sea creatures for beautiful women.

Digging deep

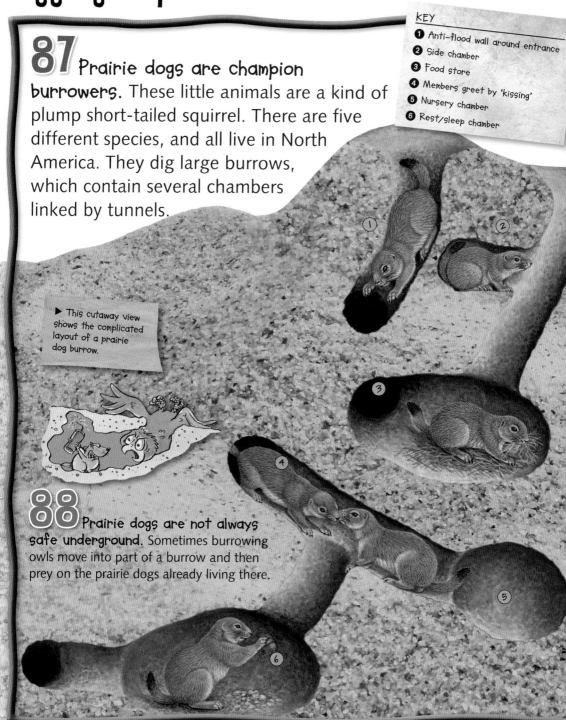

KEY
1. Anti-flood wall around entrance
2. Side chamber
3. Food store
4. Members greet by 'kissing'
5. Nursery chamber
6. Rest/sleep chamber

87 **Prairie dogs are champion burrowers.** These little animals are a kind of plump short-tailed squirrel. There are five different species, and all live in North America. They dig large burrows, which contain several chambers linked by tunnels.

▶ This cutaway view shows the complicated layout of a prairie dog burrow.

88 **Prairie dogs are not always safe underground.** Sometimes burrowing owls move into part of a burrow and then prey on the prairie dogs already living there.

40

89 Badgers dig a network of chambers and tunnels called a sett. There are special areas for breeding, sleeping and food stores. Sleeping areas are lined with dry grass and leaves, which the badgers sometimes take outside to air for a while.

▼ Badgers usually stay in their burrow during the day and come out at dusk. They are playful creatures and adults are often seen playing with their cubs.

▼ The star-nosed mole's sensitive feelers find prey by touch.

90 Moles have specially adapted front feet for digging. The feet are broad and turn outward for pushing through the soil, and the claws are large and strong. Moles have very poor sight. Their sense of touch is well developed and they have sensitive bristles on their faces.

Mothers and babies

91 Most whales are born tail first. If the baby emerged head first it could drown during the birth process. As soon as the baby has fully emerged, the mother, with the help of other females, gently pushes it up to the surface to take its first breath. The female whale feeds her baby on milk, just like other mammals.

▼ For the first months of its life, a young whale, such as this grey whale calf, remains almost touching its mother.

92 Whales are the biggest of all mammal babies. A newborn grey whale is 4 metres long, weighs two-thirds of a tonne, and drinks 200 litres of its mother's milk every day – over two bathtubs full!

93 The Virginia opossum may have more than 15 babies at one time – more than any other mammal. The young are only a centimetre long, and all of the babies together weigh only a couple of grams.

MAMMALS

94 Bears have some of the smallest babies, compared to the mother's size, of all placental mammals. A newborn giant panda weighs just 120 grams, while its mother can weigh up to 120 kilograms – 1000 times heavier. The length of pregnancy for the mother sloth bear is about seven months. Like other bears, she usually has just one or two offspring in each litter.

◄ A mother sloth bear carries her young on her back until they are perhaps one year old.

96 Baby mammals need lots of care. The young of many hunting mammals, from tiny weasels to wolves, bears and the biggest cats, are born furless, helpless, and unable to see and hear properly. The mother keeps them safe in a nest or den and returns between hunting to provide milk.

95 Some babies have to be up and running less than an hour after birth. If the young of animals such as antelopes were as helpless as the baby panda they would immediately be snapped up by predators. They must get to their feet and be able to move with the herd as quickly as possible or they will not survive.

► A newborn bison struggles to its feet minutes after birth – wolves or cougars may be near.

BIRDS

97 **A bird has two legs, a pair of wings and a body that is covered with feathers.** Birds are one of the types of animals we see most often in the wild. They live all over the world – everywhere from Antarctica to the hottest deserts. They range in size from the huge ostrich, which can be up to 2.75 metres tall, to the tiny bee hummingbird, which is scarcely bigger than a real bee.

▲ Baya weaver birds are found across South and Southeast Asia. As their name suggests, weaver birds build nests by weaving together strips of plant material and leaves.

The bird world

98 There are over 9000 different types, or species, of bird. These have been organized by scientists into 29 groups called orders, which contain many different species. The largest is the Passeriformes order.

▼ This chaffinch is in the Passeriformes order. More than half of all bird species belong to this order.

Crown

Wings

Bill, or beak

Throat

Passeriformes order:
Includes robins, sparrows and wrens

Breast

Tail

Toes

Two legs

Common swift

Apodiformes order:
Swifts and hummingbirds

Keel-billed toucan

Piciformes order:
Toucans and woodpeckers

Blue-and-yellow macaw

Psittaciformes order:
Parrots, cockatoos and lorikeets

Pied avocet

Charadriiformes order:
Waders, gulls and auks

▲ The shape of a bird's beak can be used to decide which order a bird belongs to. These pictures show examples from the largest orders.

99 All birds have wings. These are the bird's front limbs. There are many different wing shapes. Birds that soar in the sky for hours, such as eagles, have long, broad wings. These help them use air currents. Small, fast-flying birds such as swifts have slim, pointed wings.

▶ Feathers have different shapes, sizes and textures, suited to the jobs they do.

Tail feather

Flight feather

Contour (body) feather

Down feather

100 Birds are the only creatures that have feathers. They are made of keratin – the same material as our hair and nails. Feathers keep a bird warm, and its wing and tail feathers help it to fly. Some birds have colourful feathers to help attract mates or blend in with their surroundings – camouflage.

101

All birds have a beak, or bill, for eating. The beak is made of bone and is covered with a hard material called horn. Birds have different kinds of beak for different types of food. Insect-eating birds tend to have thin, sharp beaks for picking up their tiny prey. The parrot's strong beak is ideal for cracking nuts. Hunting birds, such as goshawks, have powerful hooked beaks for tearing flesh.

102

Birds lay eggs. It would be impossible for birds to carry their developing young inside their bodies like mammals do – they would be too heavy to fly.

▼ The egg protects the growing chick and provides it with food. While the young develop, the parent birds, such as this common eider, keep the eggs safe and warm. This is called incubation.

47

Big to tiny

103 The world's largest bird is the ostrich. This long-legged bird stands up to 2.75 metres tall and weighs up to 115 kilograms – twice as much as an average adult human. Males are slightly larger than females. The ostrich lives mainly on the grasslands of Africa where it feeds on plant material such as leaves, flowers and seeds.

▶ This male ostrich is looking after his chicks. Females are smaller than males and have brown feathers.

104 The bee hummingbird is the world's smallest bird. Its body, including its tail, is about 5 centimetres long and it weighs only 2 grams – about the same as a small spoonful of rice. It lives on Caribbean islands, particularly Cuba, and feeds on flower nectar like other hummingbirds.

◀ A tiny bee hummingbird eats half its weight in food every day.

105 The heaviest flying bird is the great bustard. The male weighs about 12 kilograms, although the female is slightly smaller. The bustard is a strong flier, but spends much of its life on the ground.

106 Wilson's storm petrel is the smallest seabird in the world. Only 16–19 centimetres long, this petrel hops over the surface of the water snatching up tiny sea creatures to eat. It is very common over the Atlantic, Indian and Antarctic Oceans.

107

The wandering albatross has the longest wings of any bird. When outstretched, they can measure as much as 3.6 metres from tip to tip. The albatross spends most of its life in the air. It flies over the oceans, snatching fish and squid from the water's surface.

▲ The wandering albatross only comes to land at breeding time. It lays its eggs on islands in the South Pacific, South Atlantic and Indian Oceans.

109

One of the smallest birds of prey is the collared falconet. This little bird, which lives in India and Southeast Asia, is only about 17 centimetres long. It hunts insects and other small birds.

108

The largest bird of prey is the Andean condor. A type of vulture, this bird measures about 110 centimetres in length and weighs up to 12 kilograms. It soars over the Andes Mountains of South America, hunting for food such as the remains of sheep, cows and llamas.

► The collared falconet lives in forests. Its small size helps it to fly quickly between trees.

► Andean condors often perch in tall trees and on cliffs.

Fast movers

110 **The fastest flying bird is the peregrine falcon.** It hunts other birds in the air and makes spectacular high-speed dives to catch its prey. During a hunting dive, a peregrine may reach speeds of 200 kilometres an hour. In normal level flight, it flies at about 100 kilometres an hour. Peregrine falcons live almost everywhere in the world.

Wings are bent for a high-speed dive

▶ When a peregrine falcon spots its prey, it enters into an incrediby fast, powerful dive, called a stoop.

Long slender beak reaches inside a flower to drink nectar

▶ The hummingbird's fast-beating wings make a low buzzing or humming sound that gives these birds their name.

111 **A hummingbird's wings beat 50 or more times a second as it hovers in the air.** The tiny horned sungem hummingbird beats its wings at an amazing 90 beats per second. When hovering, the hummingbird holds its body upright and beats its wings backwards and forwards.

Large, fan-shaped tail

112 Ducks and geese are also fast fliers. Many of them can fly at speeds of more than 65 kilometres an hour. The red-breasted merganser and the common eider duck can fly at up to 100 kilometres an hour.

▲ The male common eider has a distinctive patch of green feathers on the back of its neck.

113 The swift spends nearly all its life in the air and rarely comes to land. After leaving its nest, a young swift can fly up to 500,000 kilometres, and may not come to land again for two years. The common swift has been recorded flying at 112 kilometres an hour.

Swifts have long, slim wings that are perfect for their life in the air

▲ The swift can eat, drink, catch prey and mate on the wing.

114 The greater roadrunner is a fast mover on land. It runs at speeds of up to 27 kilometres an hour as it hunts for insects, lizards and birds' eggs to eat. It can fly but seems to prefer running or walking.

FEED THE BIRDS!

You will need:
225g of fat (suet, lard or dripping)
500g of seeds, nuts, biscuit crumbs, cake and other scraps   a piece of string
Ask an adult for help. Melt the fat, and mix it with the seeds and scraps. Pour it into an old yogurt pot and leave it to cool and harden. Remove the 'cake' and make a hole through it. Push the string through the hole and knot one end. Hang it from a tree, and watch as birds flock to eat it.

Superb swimmers

115 **Penguins are the best swimmers and divers in the bird world.** They live mostly in and around the Antarctic, at the very south of the world. They spend most of their lives in water, where they catch fish and tiny animals called krill to eat, but they do come to land to breed. Their wings act as strong flippers to push them through the water, and their tail and webbed feet help them to steer. Penguins sometimes get around on land by sliding over ice on their tummies!

▼ King penguins regularly dive to around 50 metres, but will sometimes go as deep as 300 metres, especially when food is scarce.

116 **The gentoo penguin is one of the fastest swimming birds.** It can swim at up to 36 kilometres an hour – faster than most people can run! Mostly, though, penguins probably swim at about 5 to 10 kilometres an hour.

▶ Gentoos race to shore then leap onto land using the surf to help them 'fly'.

117 The gannet makes an amazing dive from a height of 30 metres above the sea to catch fish. This seabird spots its prey as it soars above the ocean. Then with wings swept back and neck and beak held straight out in front, the gannet plunges like a dive-bomber. It enters the water, seizes its prey and surfaces a few seconds later.

▲ As a gannet plunges into water it must keep its eyes focused on its fast-moving prey.

QUIZ

1. Where do penguins breed – on land or in the water?
2. How fast can a gentoo penguin swim?
3. How deep do king penguins regularly dive?
4. From how high does a gannet dive?

Answers:
1. On land
2. Up to 36 kilometres an hour
3. Around 50 metres
4. 30 metres

Looking good

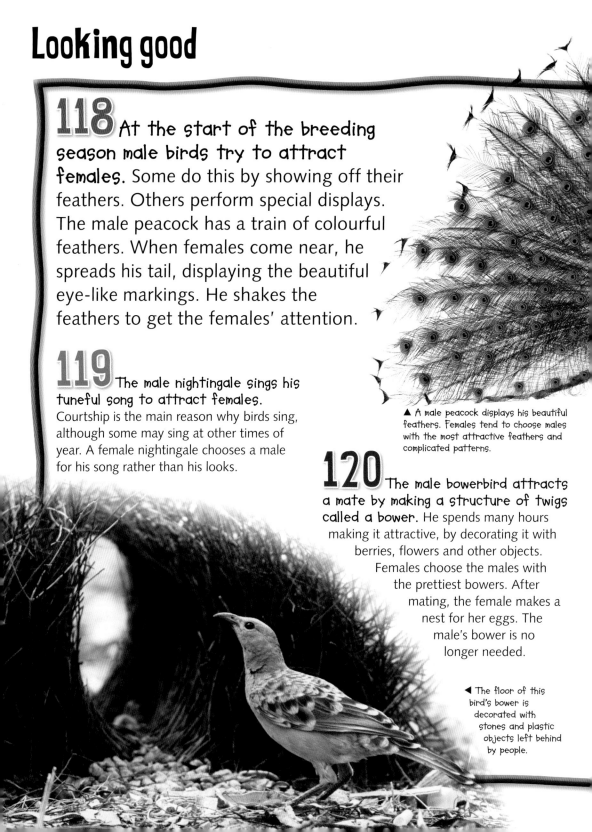

118 At the start of the breeding season male birds try to attract females. Some do this by showing off their feathers. Others perform special displays. The male peacock has a train of colourful feathers. When females come near, he spreads his tail, displaying the beautiful eye-like markings. He shakes the feathers to get the females' attention.

119 The male nightingale sings his tuneful song to attract females. Courtship is the main reason why birds sing, although some may sing at other times of year. A female nightingale chooses a male for his song rather than his looks.

▲ A male peacock displays his beautiful feathers. Females tend to choose males with the most attractive feathers and complicated patterns.

120 The male bowerbird attracts a mate by making a structure of twigs called a bower. He spends many hours making it attractive, by decorating it with berries, flowers and other objects. Females choose the males with the prettiest bowers. After mating, the female makes a nest for her eggs. The male's bower is no longer needed.

◄ The floor of this bird's bower is decorated with stones and plastic objects left behind by people.

122 The male roller performs a special display flight to impress his mate. Starting high in the air, he tumbles and rolls down to the ground while the female watches from a perch. Rollers are brightly coloured insect-eating birds.

123 Male cocks-of-the-rock dance to attract mates. Some of the most brightly coloured birds in the world, they gather in groups and leap up and down to show off their plumage to admiring females. They live in the South American rainforest.

◀ A dazzling display by the male will hopefully impress a female blue bird of paradise.

▼ Male cocks-of-the-rock fight to win a female's attention.

121 The blue bird of paradise hangs upside-down to show off his feathers. As he hangs, his tail feathers spread out and he swings backwards and forwards while making a special call to attract the attention of females. Most birds of paradise live in New Guinea. All the males have beautiful plumage, but females are much plainer.

Night birds

124 **The barn owl is adapted for hunting at night.** Its large eyes are sensitive to dim light. Its ears can pinpoint the tiniest sound and help it to find prey. The fluffy edges of the owl's feathers soften the sound of wing beats so it can swoop silently.

▼ With its pale feathers, the barn owl is a ghostly night-time hunter.

The wings are held high as the bird reaches to grab its prey

125 **Some birds, such as the poorwill, hunt insects at night when there is less competition for prey.** The poorwill sleeps during the day and wakes up at dusk to start hunting. As it flies, it opens its beak very wide and snaps moths out of the air.

An owl's clawed feet are called talons

126 **Like bats, the oilbird of South America uses sounds to help it fly in darkness.** As it flies, it makes clicking noises that bounce off obstacles in the caves in which it lives, such as the cave walls, which help the bird find its way. At night, the oilbird leaves the caves to feed on the fruits of palm trees.

The tail is tipped forwards to slow the bird as it lands

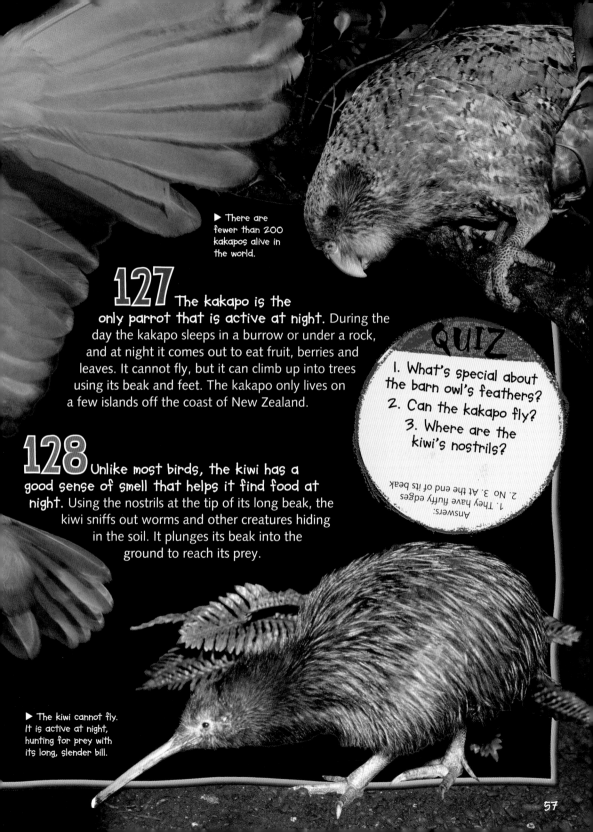

▶ There are fewer than 200 kakapos alive in the world.

127 The kakapo is the only parrot that is active at night. During the day the kakapo sleeps in a burrow or under a rock, and at night it comes out to eat fruit, berries and leaves. It cannot fly, but it can climb up into trees using its beak and feet. The kakapo only lives on a few islands off the coast of New Zealand.

128 Unlike most birds, the kiwi has a good sense of smell that helps it find food at night. Using the nostrils at the tip of its long beak, the kiwi sniffs out worms and other creatures hiding in the soil. It plunges its beak into the ground to reach its prey.

QUIZ

1. What's special about the barn owl's feathers?
2. Can the kakapo fly?
3. Where are the kiwi's nostrils?

Answers:
1. They have fluffy edges
2. No 3. At the end of its beak

▶ The kiwi cannot fly. It is active at night, hunting for prey with its long, slender bill.

Home sweet home

129 Birds make nests in which to lay their eggs. The bald eagle makes one of the biggest nests of any bird. It is made mainly of sticks and is built in a tall tree or on rocks. It is used year after year. It can be as large as 2.5 metres across and 3.5 metres deep – big enough to fit several people!

▲ A male great hornbill brings food to his mate while she incubates the eggs.

130 The female hornbill lays her eggs in prison! After finding a big enough tree hole, the female seals herself inside. She blocks the entrance to the hole with mud, leaving only a small opening. The female looks after the eggs and the male brings food, passing it through the opening.

◀ Young bald eagles rely on their parents to feed them until they are several months old.

▼ A male weaver bird often builds his nest above water. He may build more than one nest, because he can have several mates.

② Then he makes a roof, and an entrance so he can get inside

③ When it's finished, the long entrance helps to provide a safe shelter for the eggs

① The male weaver bird twists strips of leaves around a branch or twig

131 The male weaver bird makes a nest from grass, stems and leaves. He knots and weaves the pieces together to make a long nest, which hangs from the branch of a tree. The nest makes a warm, cosy home for the eggs and young, and is also very hard for any predator to get into.

132 The malleefowl makes a temperature-controlled nest mound. It is made of plants covered with sand. As the plants rot, the inside of the mound gets warmer. The eggs are laid in the sides of the mound. The male keeps a check on the temperature with his beak. If the mound cools, he adds sand. If it gets too hot he makes some openings to let warmth out.

133 The female cuckoo doesn't make a nest at all — she lays her eggs in the nests of other birds! She lays up to 12 eggs, all in different nests. The owner of the nest is called the host bird. The cuckoo removes one of the host bird's eggs before laying one of her own, so the number in the nest remains the same.

134 The cave swiftlet makes a nest from its own saliva or spit. It uses the spit as glue to make a cup-shaped nest of feathers and grass.

Great travellers

135 The Canada goose spends summer in the Arctic and flies south in winter. This regular journey is called a migration. In summer, the Arctic blooms and there is food for the geese to eat while they rear their young. In autumn, when the weather turns colder, they migrate to warmer climates farther south. This means the bird gets warmer weather all year round.

Arctic

Southern North America

▶ Canada geese fly southwards before breeding.

▶ The Arctic tern travels farther than any other bird and sees more hours of daylight each year than any other creature.

Arctic

136 The Arctic tern makes one of the longest migrations of any bird. It breeds in the Arctic during the northern summer. Then, as winter approaches, the tern makes the long journey south to the Antarctic – a trip of some 15,000 kilometres – where it catches the southern summer. The tern gets the benefit of long daylight hours for feeding all year round.

Antarctic

▼ Some flocks of Canada geese make journeys of 1500 kilometres.

137 Migrating birds can use landmarks, the position of the Sun when it sets and even the Earth's magnetic field to help them navigate.

Arctic

Southern South America

▲ American golden plovers make some of the longest journeys of any animal.

138 Every autumn, the American golden plover flies up to 12,800 kilometres from North to South America. It breeds on the North American tundra where it feasts on the insects that fill the air during the brief Arctic summer. When summer is over the plover flies to the grasslands of southern South America for the winter. This means it has plentiful food supplies all year round.

Desert birds

139 The elf owl makes its nest in a hole in a desert cactus. This prickly, uncomfortable home helps to keep the owl's eggs safe from predators that do not want to struggle through the cactus' spines.

▶ The elf owl is one of the smallest owls in the world and is only about 14 centimetres long. It lives in desert areas in the southwest USA.

I DON'T BELIEVE IT!

The lammergeier vulture drops bones onto rocks to smash them. It then eats the soft marrow and even splinters of bone. Acids in the bird's stomach can digest the bone.

140 Desert birds may have to travel long distances to find water. This is not always possible for chicks. To solve this problem, the male sandgrouse has feathers on his tummy that act like sponges to hold water. He soaks his feathers, and then flies back to his young, which gulp down the water that he's brought.

◀ The sandgrouse lives throughout Asia, often in semi-desert areas.

141 Many desert birds have very light, sandy-brown feathers to blend with their surroundings. The cream-coloured courser lives in deserts in Africa and Asia. It searches for prey on the ground, as when it flies, the black-and-white pattern on the underside of its wings makes it easier for predators to spot.

◄ A cactus wren rarely needs to drink water. It can get most of what it needs from its food.

142 The lappet-faced vulture scavenges for its food. It glides over the deserts of Africa and the Middle East, searching for dead animals. The vulture attacks a carcass with its strong hooked bill. Its head and neck are bare so it does not have to clean its feathers after feeding from a messy carcass.

143 The cactus wren eats cactus fruits and berries. This little bird hops among the spines of cactus plants in search of juicy morsels. It also catches insects, small lizards and frogs. Cactus wrens live in the southwestern USA.

▼ The lappet-faced vulture is the largest vulture in Africa. It is strong enough to fight off other birds and even mammals such as jackals, and its large beak can rip through skin and muscle.

Staying safe

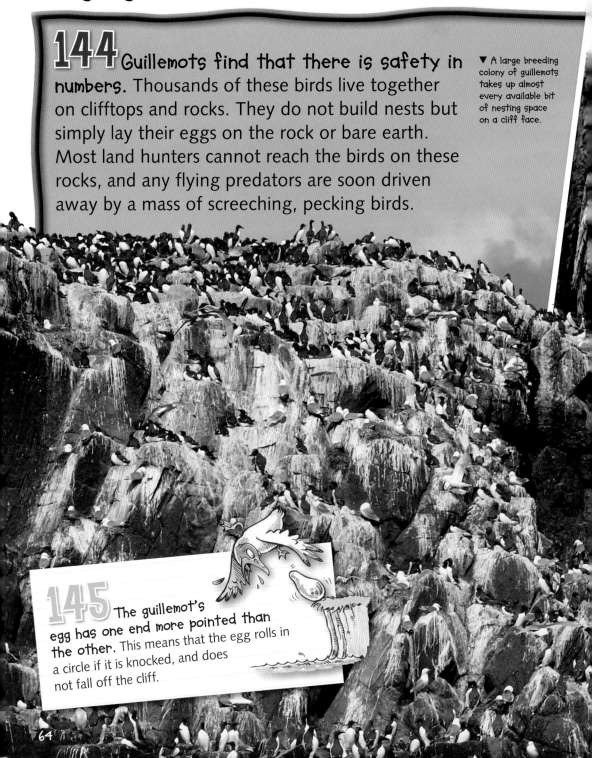

144 Guillemots find that there is safety in numbers. Thousands of these birds live together on clifftops and rocks. They do not build nests but simply lay their eggs on the rock or bare earth. Most land hunters cannot reach the birds on these rocks, and any flying predators are soon driven away by a mass of screeching, pecking birds.

▼ A large breeding colony of guillemots takes up almost every available bit of nesting space on a cliff face.

145 The guillemot's egg has one end more pointed than the other. This means that the egg rolls in a circle if it is knocked, and does not fall off the cliff.

146 Birds have clever ways of hiding themselves from predators. The tawny frogmouth is an Australian bird that hunts at night. During the day, it rests in trees where its brownish, mottled feathers make it hard to see. If the bird senses danger it stretches itself, with its beak pointing upwards, so that it looks almost exactly like a broken branch or tree stump.

147 If a predator comes too close to her young, the female killdeer leads it away using a clever trick. She moves away from the nest, which is made on the ground, making sure the predator has noticed her. She then starts to drag one wing as though she is injured and is easy prey. When she has lead the predator far enough away, the killdeer suddenly flies away.

◀ Tawny frogmouths can blend in well, despite being large birds. They can grow to 50 centimetres long.

▶ A female killdeer imitates an injured wing to lead a predator away from her nest.

Amazing eggs

148 A bird's egg protects the developing chick inside. The yellow yolk in the egg provides the chick with food. Layers of egg white, called albumen, cushion the chick and keep it warm, and also supply it with food. The hard shell keeps everything safe. The shell is porous – it allows air in and out so that the chick can breathe. The parent birds incubate the egg in the nest.

149 The number of eggs laid in a clutch varies from one to more than 20. A clutch is the name for the number of eggs that a bird lays in one go. The number of clutches per year also changes from bird to bird. The grey partridge lays one of the biggest clutches, with an average of 15 to 19 eggs. The emperor penguin lays just one egg a year.

▼ The egg protects and nourishes the chick as it develops.

① The chick is beginning to form. It is nourished by the yolk.

Yolk sac contains food

② The chick's tiny wings and legs are beginning to grow.

Strong shell has pores (tiny holes) to allow air to pass through

Developing chick

'Egg tooth'

③ Soon the chick's body will take up all the space inside the egg.

④ The chick uses an 'egg tooth' to peck at the shell so it can hatch.

Egg white supplies proteins, water and vitamins

150 The ostrich egg is the biggest in the world. It weighs about 1.5 kilograms – an average hen's egg weighs only about 50 grams. The shell of the ostrich egg is very strong, measuring up to 2 millimetres thick. A female ostrich can lay up to 11 enormous eggs at a time. However, the ostrich egg is actually the smallest when compared to the size of the parent bird.

◄ An ostrich egg measures 16 centimetres in length.

151 The smallest egg in the world is laid by the bee hummingbird. The delicate egg is laid in a cup-shaped nest of cobwebs and plants. It weighs about 0.3 grams. The bird itself weighs only 2 grams.

◄ The bee hummingbird egg is just 6 millimetres in length.

152 The kiwi lays an egg a quarter of her own size. The egg weighs 420 grams – the kiwi itself weighs only 1.7 kilograms. This is equivalent to a new human baby weighing 17.5 kilograms – most weigh about 3.5 kilograms.

153 The great spotted woodpecker incubates its egg for only ten days. This is one of the shortest incubation periods of any bird. The longest is of the wandering albatross, which incubates its eggs for up to 82 days.

QUIZ

1. Which part of the egg cushions the chick?
2. How many eggs a year does the emperor penguin lay?
3. How much does the bee hummingbird's egg weigh?
4. For how long does the wandering albatross incubate its eggs?

Answers:
1. The egg white (albumen)
2. One 3. 0.3 grams
4. Up to 82 days

► A female great spotted woodpecker feeds a juicy caterpillar to her hungry chick. Once a chick has hatched it needs a lot of food.

Hunters and scavengers

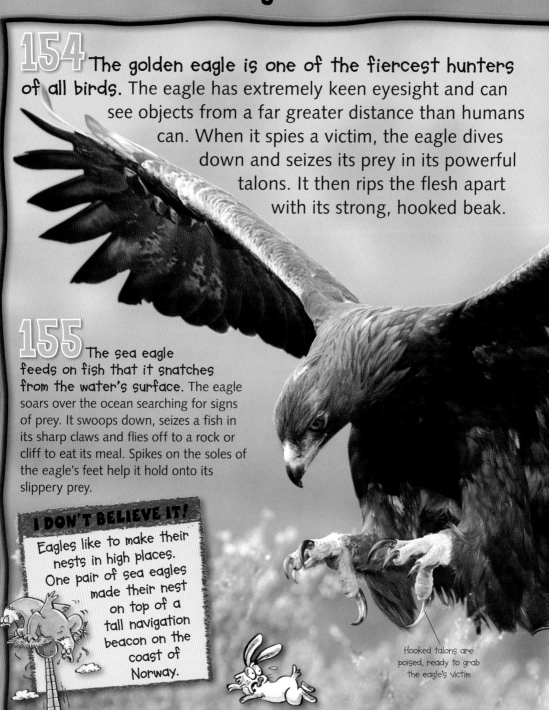

154 **The golden eagle is one of the fiercest hunters of all birds.** The eagle has extremely keen eyesight and can see objects from a far greater distance than humans can. When it spies a victim, the eagle dives down and seizes its prey in its powerful talons. It then rips the flesh apart with its strong, hooked beak.

155 **The sea eagle feeds on fish that it snatches from the water's surface.** The eagle soars over the ocean searching for signs of prey. It swoops down, seizes a fish in its sharp claws and flies off to a rock or cliff to eat its meal. Spikes on the soles of the eagle's feet help it hold onto its slippery prey.

I DON'T BELIEVE IT!

Eagles like to make their nests in high places. One pair of sea eagles made their nest on top of a tall navigation beacon on the coast of Norway.

Hooked talons are poised, ready to grab the eagle's victim

A single wing feather can be 35 to 50 centimetres long

◀ The golden eagle can soar for hours, searching for prey such as rabbits and other birds.

156 The raven is one of the biggest songbirds and a powerful hunter. It grows up to 63 centimetres long, has a strong beak and can run fast on the ground as well as fly. Rats and mice are its main prey, but it can even kill a creature as large as a rabbit. Ravens also scavenge, eating animals that are already dead or the kills of other hunters.

▶ Ravens look like crows, but their beaks are bigger and stronger.

Tail feathers are unusually long – up to 35 centimetres

Caring for the young

157 Emperor penguins have the worst breeding conditions of any bird. They lay eggs and rear their young on the Antarctic ice. The female penguin lays one egg at the start of the Antarctic winter. She returns to the sea, leaving her partner to incubate it on his feet. The egg is covered by a flap of the male's skin, which keeps it warm.

158 Hawks and falcons look after their young and bring them food for many weeks. Their chicks are born blind and helpless. They are totally dependent on their parents for food and protection until they grow large enough to hunt for themselves.

▶ When the chick hatches, the female penguin returns while the hungry male finds food. Emperor penguin chicks sit on their parents' feet to keep off the frozen ground.

▼ Peregrine falcon parents normally care for two to four chicks at a time.

159 Pigeons feed their young on 'pigeon milk'. This special liquid is made in the lining of part of the bird's throat, called the crop. The young birds are fed on this for the first few days of their lives and then start to eat seeds and other solid food.

160
Some birds, such as ducks and geese, are able to move around as soon as they hatch. Ducklings follow the first moving thing they see – usually their mother. This is called imprinting. It is a form of learning that can happen only in the first few hours of an animal's life. It ensures that the young birds stay close to their mother.

▼ These mallard chicks stand a greater chance of survival by staying close to their mother.

161
Young birds must learn their songs from adults. A young bird such as a chaffinch is born being able to make sounds. But, like a human baby learning to speak, it has to learn the chaffinch song by listening to its parents and practising.

162
Swans carry their young on their back as they swim. This allows the parent bird to move fast without having to wait for the young, called cygnets, to keep up. When the cygnets are riding on the parent bird's back they are safe from predators.

▼ A female mute swan and cygnets. Both parents take turns to care for the young.

Birds of the jungle

163 Birds of paradise are among the most colourful of all rainforest birds. The males have brilliant plumage and decorative feathers. There are about 42 different kinds and all live in the forests of New Guinea and northeast Australia. Fruit is their main source of food, but some feed on insects.

164 The scarlet macaw is one of the largest parrots in the world. It is an incredible 85 centimetres long, including its impressive tail, and lives in the South American rainforest. It moves in large flocks that screech as they fly from tree to tree, feeding on fruit and leaves.

◀ Parrots, such as the scarlet macaw, have hooked beaks that they use to crack nuts, open seeds and tear at fruit.

165 The junglefowl is the wild ancestor of the farmyard chicken. This colourful bird lives in the rainforests of Southeast Asia, where it feeds on seeds and insects.

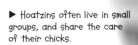

▶ Hoatzins often live in small groups, and share the care of their chicks.

166 The hoatzin builds its nest overhanging water. If its chicks are in danger from predators they can escape by dropping into the water and swimming to safety. This strange bird with its ragged crest lives in the Amazon rainforest.

167 The Congo peafowl was only discovered in 1936. It lives in the dense rainforest of West Africa and is rarely seen. The male bird has beautiful glossy feathers of green, violet-blue and red, while the female is mostly brown and green.

▼ Harpy eagles perch on high branches to get a good view of the forest below.

168 The harpy eagle is the world's largest eagle. It is about 90 centimetres long and has huge feet and long, sharp claws. It feeds on rainforest animals such as monkeys and sloths.

◀ Quetzals can perch without moving a muscle, making themselves hard to spot in the rainforest.

169 The male resplendant quetzal has magnificent tail feathers, which are up to 90 centimetres long. This beautiful bird lives in the rainforests of Mexico and South America. It was worshipped as a sacred bird by the ancient Mayan and Aztec people.

Flightless birds

170 The fast-running emu is the largest bird native to Australia. Like the ostrich it cannot fly, but it can run at speeds of up to 50 kilometres an hour. Most flightless birds need speed to avoid being caught by predators. They have long legs, packed with muscles. Ostriches and emus can also deliver a mighty kick if they are scared.

▲ Emus can only run at top speed for a short time. They are hunted by wild dogs, eagles and crocodiles.

171 One rhea egg is the equivalent in size to about 12 hen's eggs. It has long been a tasty feast for local people.

▶ The ostrich is the world's fastest two-legged runner. It is specially adapted for speed, and can run at up to 70 kilometres an hour.

Very powerful upper leg muscles

Extra flexible ankles

Penguins can waddle, run and jump, and are very strong swimmers

Kiwis rely on the cover of darkness, not speed, to stay safe

Roadrunners can reach speeds of 32 kilometres an hour, and they can also fly a little

▲ There are about 40 different types of flightless birds alive today, which have various ways of staying safe.

172 The speedy rhea lives on the grassy plains of South America. In the breeding season, males fight to gather a flock of females. Once he has his flock, the winning male digs a nest. Each of the females lays her eggs in this nest. The male incubates them, and looks after the chicks until they are about six months old.

▲ The rhea can sprint faster than a horse, reaching speeds of up to 50 kilometres an hour.

Long, strong legs

Bendy two-toed feet

173 Cassowaries are flightless birds that live in the rainforests of Australia and New Guinea. There are three species – all are large birds with long, strong legs and big, sharp-clawed feet. On the cassowary's head is a large horny crest, called a casque. Experts are not sure why cassowaries have casques, but they may be useful in making, and hearing, low booming calls that can be heard in the dense forest.

On the river

174 Kingfishers live close to rivers, where they hunt for fish. At breeding time, a pair of birds tunnels into the riverbank, using their strong beaks. They prepare a nesting chamber at the end of the long tunnel. Here the female can safely lay up to eight eggs. Both parents look after the eggs, and feed the chicks when they hatch.

▶ A kingfisher plunges into the water, grabbing a fish in its dagger-like beak.

▼ Ospreys are also known as 'fish hawks'. As they dive into the water, they keep the prey in their sights.

175 The osprey is a bird of prey that feeds mainly on fish. This bird is found almost all over the world near rivers and lakes. It watches for prey from the air then plunges into the water with its feet held out in front. Special spikes on the soles of its feet help it hold onto its slippery catch.

176 The pelican collects fish in the big pouch that hangs beneath its long beak. When the pelican pushes its beak into the water the pouch stretches and fills with water, scooping up fish. When the pelican lifts its head up, the water drains out of the pouch leaving the food behind.

▲ A pelican's massive pouch works like a fishing net to trap prey.

178 The heron catches fish and other creatures such as insects and frogs. This long-legged bird stands on the shore or in shallow water and grabs its prey with a swift thrust of its sharp beak.

179 A small bird called the dipper is well-adapted to river life. It usually lives around fast-flowing streams and can swim and dive well. It can even walk along the bottom of a stream, snapping up prey such as insects and other small creatures. There are five different types of dipper and they live in North and South America, Asia and Europe.

▶ An African jacana feeds from water lettuce on the head of a hippopotamus.

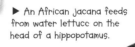

177 The jacana can walk on water! It has amazingly long toes that spread the bird's weight over a large area. This allows it to walk on floating lily pads as it hunts for food such as insects. Jacanas can also swim and dive. There are eight different types of jacana, also called lilytrotters.

Finding food

180 **The woodpecker uses its strong beak to bore into tree trunks and catch insects.** The bird holds on to a tree trunk using its strong feet and sharp claws. Its stiff tail feathers also provide support. It hammers into the trunk, disturbing wood-boring insects that live beneath the bark. The woodpecker quickly snaps up the escaping insects.

181 **The honeyguide bird uses the honey badger to help it get to its food.** Found in parts of Africa and Asia, the honeyguide feeds on bee grubs and honey. It is not strong enough to break into bees' nests, so it leads the honey badger towards them. When the honey badger smashes into the nest, the honeyguide can also eat its fill.

◄ Woodpeckers also use their beaks to make nest holes in tree trunks, like this red-bellied woodpecker.

▲ Ocellated antbirds have a 'tooth' at the tip of the beak, for crushing insects.

182 The antbird keeps watch over army ants as they march through the forest. The bird flies just ahead of the ants and perches on a low branch. It then pounces on the insects, spiders and other small creatures that try to escape from the column of ants. Some antbirds also eat the ants. Antbirds live in North and South America.

183 The hummingbird has to eat lots of nectar to get enough energy to survive. If a human were to work as hard as a hummingbird, he or she would need to eat three times their weight in potatoes each day.

184 The hummingbird feeds on flower nectar. Nectar is a sweet liquid made by flowers to attract pollinating insects. It is not always easy for birds to reach, but the hummingbird is able to hover in front of the flower while it sips the nectar using its long tongue.

▲ Colourful flowers and sweet perfumes attract nectar feeders, such as hummingbirds.

Winter birds

185 **The coldest places on Earth are the Arctic and the Antarctic.** The Arctic is at the most northern point of the Earth, and the Antarctic is at the far south. The snowy owl is one of the largest birds in the Arctic. Its white feathers help to camouflage it in the snow.

Dark bars on a female's feathers help her to hide when she is nesting among snowy rocks

186 **Penguins have a thick layer of fat just under their skin to help protect them from the cold.** Their feathers are waterproof and very tightly packed for warmth. Penguins live mainly in Antarctica, but some live in parts of South Africa, South America and Australia.

▶ Snowy owls ambush their prey, approaching with almost silent wing beats.

187 **In winter, the ptarmigan has white feathers to help it hide from predators in the Arctic snow.** But in summer its white plumage would make it very easy to spot, so the ptarmigan moults and grows brown and grey feathers instead.

Summer plumage

Winter plumage

◀ Rock ptarmigans are stocky birds that feed on plants at ground level.

▲ Bewick swans care for their young throughout their first winter, and sometimes for a second winter too.

188 The Bewick swan lays its eggs and rears its young on the tundra of the Arctic. The female bird makes a nest on the ground and lays up to five eggs. Both parents care for the young. In autumn the family travels south to warmer lands.

189 Sheathbills are scavengers and will eat almost anything they can find. These large white birds live on islands close to the Antarctic. They do catch fish but they also search the beaches for any dead animals. They will also snatch weak or dying young from seals and penguins.

▼ A sheathbill tries to steal food from a gentoo penguin feeding its

190 The snow bunting breeds on Arctic islands, farther north than any other bird. The female makes a nest of grasses, moss and lichens on the ground. She lays four to eight eggs and both parents help to care for the young.

Snowy owls have a wingspan of about 130 centimetres

Special beaks

191 The snail kite feeds primarily on water snails, and its curved beak is specially shaped for this diet. When the kite catches a snail, it holds it in one foot while standing on a branch or other perch. It strikes the snail's body with its sharp beak and shakes it from the shell.

▲ The snail kite is a type of hawk that lives in the southern USA, the Caribbean and South America. It is now very rare.

192 The lower half of the skimmer's beak is longer than the upper half. The skimmer flies just above the water with the lower part below the surface. When it comes across a fish, the skimmer snaps the upper part down to trap its prey.

193 The crossbill has a very unusual beak that crosses at the tip. This shape helps the bird to open up the scales of pine cones and remove the seeds that it feeds on.

◀ Male crossbills are red. Females are usually olive green or greenish-yellow, although both have dark brown wings and tail.

▶ There are sieve-like plates on the edges of a flamingo's beak. These plates help to trap the food that the bird eats.

194 The flamingo uses its beak to filter food from shallow water. It stands in the water with its head down and its beak beneath the surface. Water flows into the beak and is pushed out again by the flamingo's large tongue. Tiny animals and plants are trapped – and swallowed.

▼ This female wrybill can use her beak to reach young insects that lurk beneath pebbles.

195 The wrybill is the only bird with a beak that curves to the right. The wrybill is a type of plover that lives in New Zealand. It sweeps its beak over the ground in circles to pick up insects.

196 The toco toucan's beak is about 19 centimetres long. It helps the toucan to reach fruit and berries at the ends of branches. All toucans have large brightly coloured beaks. The different colours and patterns may help them attract mates.

▲ As well as a way of eating fruit, scientists think that a toucan's large beak may help it to lose heat when the bird is too hot.

REPTILES AND AMPHIBIANS

197 Reptiles and amphibians are cold-blooded animals. This means that they need the Sun's heat to warm them up. Reptiles spend much of their time on land, but most amphibians live in or around water.

Dry, scaly skin

Sharp claws

Smooth, moist skin

► The skin of an amphibian is smooth and moist. Most amphibians, such as this frog, have long hind legs that are ideal for jumping.

Large eyes

Long hind legs

Long toes

Four legs

Long tail

Four legs

◄ Reptiles, such as this lizard, have dry, scaly skin and are often colourful creatures. Not all reptiles have legs, but if they do, their legs are on the sides of their bodies.

Scales and slime

198 Reptiles and amphibians can be divided into smaller groups. There are four kinds of reptiles – snakes, lizards and amphisbaenians, the crocodile family, tortoises and turtles, and the tuataras. Amphibians are split into frogs and toads, newts and salamanders, and caecilians.

199 Reptiles do a lot of sunbathing! Sitting in the sun is called basking – reptiles bask to warm themselves with the Sun's heat so they can move. When it gets cold, at night or during a cold season, reptiles might hibernate, which is a type of deep sleep.

▶ Blue-collared lizards may bask for many hours at a time.

Over half of all reptiles are lizards – there are nearly 5000 species.

Amphisbaenians, or worm lizards, are burrowing reptiles that live underground.

Tuataras are rare, ancient and unusual reptiles from New Zealand.

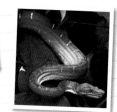

Snakes are the second largest group of reptiles.

Crocodiles, alligators, gharials and caimans are predators with sharp teeth.

Turtles and tortoises have hard shells that protect them from predators.

200 Most reptiles have dry, scaly, waterproof skin. This stops their bodies from drying out. The scales are made of keratin and may form thick, tough plates. Human nails are made of the same material.

Amphibian family

Newts have slender bodies and long tails.

Frogs have smooth skin and long legs for jumping.

Toads often have warty skin and crawl or walk.

Salamanders have tails and they usually have bright markings.

Caecilians are burrowing animals without legs.

▼ Green-skinned frogs can hide among leaves and pondweed.

201 **Amphibians have skin that is moist, smooth and soft.** Oxygen can pass easily through their skin, which is important because most adult amphibians breathe through their skin as well as with their lungs. Reptiles breathe only with their lungs.

202 **Amphibians' skin is kept moist by special glands just under the surface.** These glands produce a sticky substance called mucus. Many amphibians also keep their skin moist by making sure that they are never far away from water.

203 **Some amphibians have no lungs.** Humans breathe with their lungs to get oxygen from the air and breathe out carbon dioxide. Most amphibians breathe through their skin and lungs, but lungless salamanders breathe only through their skin and the lining of the mouth.

Sun worshippers

204 Most reptiles live in warm or hot habitats. Many are found in dry, burning-hot places such as deserts and dry grassland. They have various clever ways of surviving in these harsh conditions.

▼ Thorny devils are Australian reptiles. When it rains, water trickles along a thorny devil's back, towards its mouth!

205 Even reptiles can get too hot sometimes! When this happens, they hide in the shade of a rock or bury themselves in the sand. Some escape the heat by being nocturnal – coming out mostly at night.

206 Reptiles need very little food and water. That means they can survive in places where there are not many plants or animals to eat, such as deserts. Their thick skin has an important job to do – it stops too much water from escaping from their bodies.

▲ A spadefoot toad has strong, clawed feet for digging.

207 Reptiles need a certain level of warmth to survive. This is why there are no reptiles in very cold places, such as at the North and South Poles, or at the very tops of mountains.

208 Like reptiles, many amphibians live in very hot places. Sometimes it can get too hot and dry for them. The spadefoot toad from Europe, Asia and North America buries itself in the sand to escape the heat and dryness.

209 The sand lizard of the African Namib Desert performs strange dances. When it gets too hot, it may lift its legs up and down off the burning sand, or lie on its stomach and raise all its legs at once!

Cooler customers

210 Many amphibians are common in cooler, damper parts of the world. Amphibians like wet places. Most mate and lay their eggs in water.

▶ Frogs can hide from strong sunlight by resting in trees or under plants.

211 As spring arrives, amphibians come out of hiding. The warmer weather sees many amphibians returning to the pond or stream where they were born. This may mean a very long journey through towns or over busy roads.

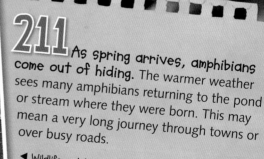

◀ Wildlife watchers help common toads cross the road to reach their breeding ponds in safety.

▲ When it is time to hibernate, a frog must find a safe, damp place to stay.

212
When the weather turns especially cold, amphibians often hide away. They simply hibernate in the mud at the bottom of ponds or under stones and logs. This means that they go to sleep in the autumn and don't wake up until spring.

Gills

▶ This is a mudpuppy — a type of salamander. It spends its whole life underwater and breathes using its frilly gills.

213
Journeys to breeding grounds may be up to 5 kilometres — a long way for an animal only a few centimetres in length. This is like a person walking 90 kilometres away without a map! The animals find their way by scent, landmarks, the Earth's magnetic field and the Sun's position.

▲ Pygmy marbled newts avoid getting too hot by hiding under rotting wood or by resting in mud during the day.

Water babies

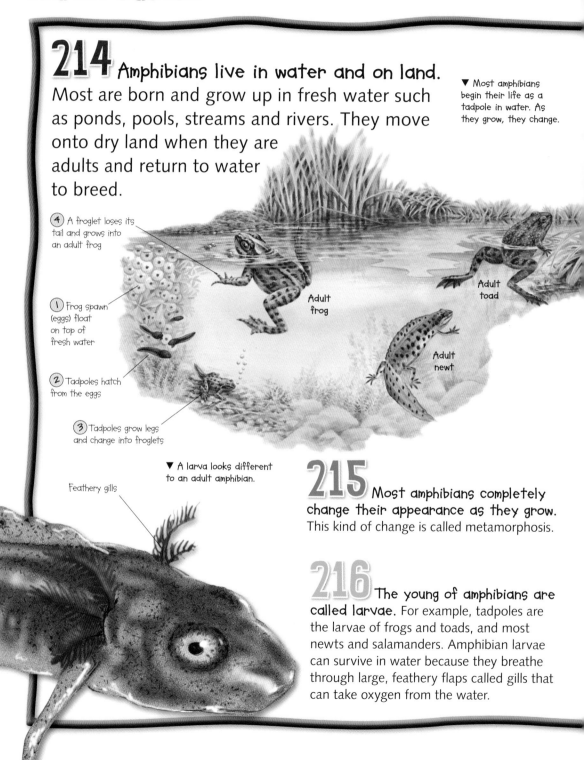

214 Amphibians live in water and on land. Most are born and grow up in fresh water such as ponds, pools, streams and rivers. They move onto dry land when they are adults and return to water to breed.

▼ Most amphibians begin their life as a tadpole in water. As they grow, they change.

4 A froglet loses its tail and grows into an adult frog

1 Frog spawn (eggs) float on top of fresh water

2 Tadpoles hatch from the eggs

3 Tadpoles grow legs and change into froglets

Adult frog

Adult toad

Adult newt

▼ A larva looks different to an adult amphibian.

Feathery gills

215 Most amphibians completely change their appearance as they grow. This kind of change is called metamorphosis.

216 The young of amphibians are called larvae. For example, tadpoles are the larvae of frogs and toads, and most newts and salamanders. Amphibian larvae can survive in water because they breathe through large, feathery flaps called gills that can take oxygen from the water.

▲ An axolotl is a strange creature that remains a tadpole all its life.

217 **The axolotl is an amphibian that has never grown up.** This type of water-living salamander has never developed beyond the larval stage. It does, however, develop far enough to be able to breed.

▼ Toads can lay hundreds – even thousands – of eggs at a time.

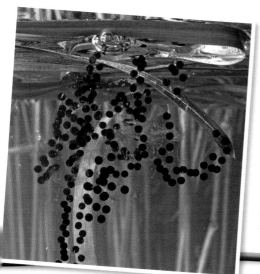

218 **The male South American Surinam toad is quite an acrobat.** When mating underwater, it has to press the eggs onto its mate's back. The eggs remain there until they hatch.

219 **The majority of amphibians lay soft eggs.** These may be in a jelly-like string or clump of tiny eggs called spawn, as with frogs and toads. Newts lay their eggs singly.

220 **A few amphibians give birth to live young instead of laying eggs.** The eggs of the fire salamander, for example, stay inside their mother, where the young hatch out and develop. The female then gives birth to young that are like miniature adults.

Land babies

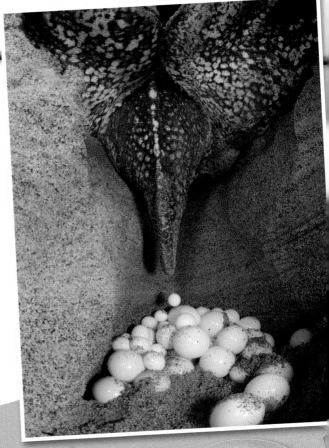

221 The majority of reptiles spend their whole lives away from water. They are very well adapted for life on dry land. Some do spend time in the water, but most reptiles lay their eggs on land.

▶ A leatherback turtle uses her hind legs to dig a burrow in the sand, and then lays her clutch of round eggs inside.

Alligator

Ground python

Javan bloodsucker lizard

Galapagos giant tortoise

▲ Reptiles lay eggs of different shapes and sizes.

222 Most reptile eggs are much tougher than those of amphibians. This is because they must survive life out of the water. Lizards and snakes lay eggs with leathery shells. Crocodile and tortoise eggs have a hard shell rather like birds' eggs.

223 The eggs feed and protect the young developing inside them. Yolk provides food for the developing young, which is called an embryo. The shell protects the embryo from the outside world, but also allows vital oxygen into the egg.

① When fully developed, a baby snake uses the egg tooth on the tip of its snout to tear a hole in the egg.

② The snake tastes the air with its forked tongue. It may stay in the shell for a few more days.

③ Eventually, the snake uncoils its body and wriggles free of the egg.

④ The baby snake slides along in S-shaped curves to begin its life in the wild.

AMAZING EGGS

Reptile eggs are like birds' eggs. Next time you eat an egg, rinse out half an empty eggshell, fill it with water and wait a while. See how no water escapes! Wash your hands well once you're done. Like this bird's eggshell, reptile eggshells stop the egg from drying out, although they let air in and are tough enough to protect the embryo.

224 Young reptiles hatch out of eggs as miniature adults. They do not undergo a change, or metamorphosis, like amphibians do.

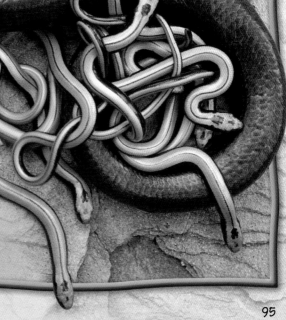

▶ A slow worm protects her eggs inside her body, until they are ready to hatch.

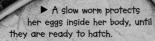

225 Some snakes and lizards, like slow worms, don't lay eggs. Instead, they give birth to fully developed live young. Animals that do this are called 'viviparous'.

Little and large

226 Reptiles and amphibians come in every shape and size. There are more than 9000 species (types) of reptiles and 7000 species of amphibians. They range from tiny frogs to giant, dinosaur-like lizards.

Chinese salamanders are
~~en~~ heavier than their
~~panese~~ cousins. They
~~n~~ weigh up to 65 kg –
~~re~~ than a child!

227 The largest reptile is the saltwater crocodile from around the Indian and west Pacific Oceans.
It can grow to a staggering 7 metres from nose to tail – an average adult human is not even 2 metres tall! Japan's cold streams are home to the largest amphibian – a giant salamander that is around 1.5 metres in length and weighs up to 40 kilograms.

▼ Most saltwater crocodiles grow to be about 5 metres in length. These massive predators are called 'salties' in Australia.

228 The world's tiniest reptiles are dwarf geckos.
The smallest one discovered so far measured just 16 millimetres in length. The Brazilian gold frog is one of the smallest amphibians. Its body length is just 9.8 millimetres – that makes it small enough to sit on your thumbnail!

▶ A European tree frog is up to 50 millimetres long.

▼ A female pygmy leaf chameleon is just 34 millimetres long, but the male is even smaller!

ACTUAL SIZE

Adaptable animals

229 Many reptiles and amphibians have special adaptations to help them live safely and easily in their surroundings. For example, crocodiles have a special flap in their throats that means that they can open their mouth underwater without breathing in water.

230 Geckos can climb up vertical surfaces or even upside down. They are able to cling on because they have five wide-spreading toes, each with sticky toe-pads, on each foot. These strong pads are covered with millions of tiny hairs that grip surfaces tightly.

◀ Tokay geckos are one of the largest geckos. They can reach up to 35 centimetres in length and are usually brightly patterned.

231 Tortoises and turtles have hard, bony shells for protection. They form a suit of armour that protects them from predators and also from the hot Sun.

LEARNING MORE

Pick a favourite reptile or amphibian and then find out as much as you can about it. List all the ways you think it is especially well adapted to deal with its lifestyle and habitat.

▶ Colourful chameleons often have a row of spines on their backs to make them look fierce.

232 **Chameleons have adapted well to their way of life in the trees.** They have long toes that can grip branches firmly, and a long tail that grips like another hand. Tails that can grip like this are called prehensile. Chameleons are also known for being able to change their colour to blend in with their surroundings. This is called camouflage, and is something that many other reptiles and amphibians use.

233 **The flattened tails of newts make them expert swimmers.** Newts are salamanders that spend most of their lives in water, so they need to be able to get about speedily in this environment.

▼ The smooth newt has a flat, paddle-like tail that helps it swim quickly as it chases prey.

234 **Some amphibians use gills to breathe underwater.** Blood flows inside the feathery gills as water flows over the outside. As the water flows past the gills, oxygen passes out of the water, straight into the blood.

Natural show-offs

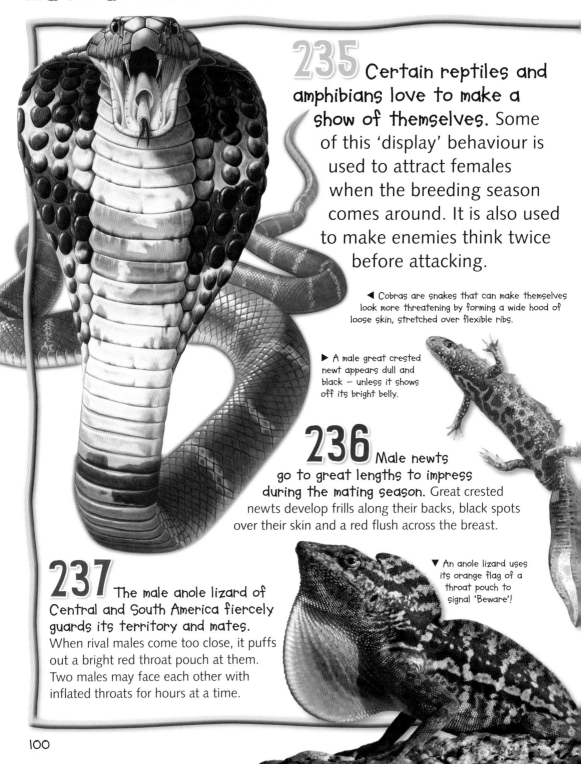

235 Certain reptiles and amphibians love to make a show of themselves. Some of this 'display' behaviour is used to attract females when the breeding season comes around. It is also used to make enemies think twice before attacking.

◀ Cobras are snakes that can make themselves look more threatening by forming a wide hood of loose skin, stretched over flexible ribs.

▶ A male great crested newt appears dull and black — unless it shows off its bright belly.

236 Male newts go to great lengths to impress during the mating season. Great crested newts develop frills along their backs, black spots over their skin and a red flush across the breast.

237 The male anole lizard of Central and South America fiercely guards its territory and mates. When rival males come too close, it puffs out a bright red throat pouch at them. Two males may face each other with inflated throats for hours at a time.

▼ An anole lizard uses its orange flag of a throat pouch to signal 'Beware'!

238
Many frogs and toads puff themselves up. Toads can inflate their bodies to appear more frightening. Frogs and toads can also puff out their throat pouches. This makes their croaking love-calls to mates and 'back off' calls to enemies much louder.

▲ A green tree frog uses its air-filled throat pouch to impress a female.

239
Some male Agamid lizards appear to impress females with body-building. They can be seen perched on top of rocks, doing push-ups and bobbing their heads up and down!

240
A frilled lizard in full display is an amazing sight. This lizard has a large flap of neck skin that normally lies flat. When faced by a predator, it spreads this out to form a huge, stiff ruff that makes the lizard look bigger and scarier!

241
Male monitor lizards have wrestling competitions! At the beginning of the mating season they compete to try to win the females. They rear up on their hind legs and wrestle until the weaker one gives up.

▲ A frilled lizard scares predators away with its huge frill, large yellow mouth and a loud hiss.

Sensitive creatures

242 Reptiles and amphibians find out about the world by using their senses, such as taste and sight. Senses tell an animal about the world around them and any deadly animals that may be lurking nearby. Good senses can also help an animal to find food and mates.

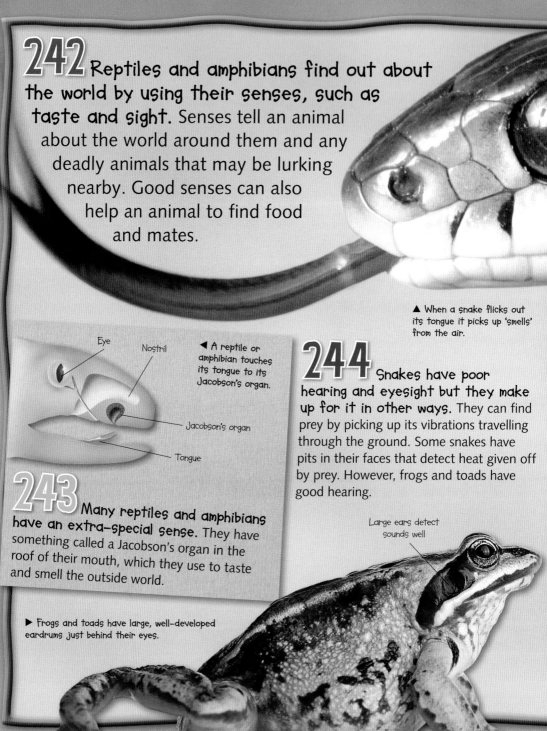

▲ When a snake flicks out its tongue it picks up 'smells' from the air.

Eye

Nostril

◀ A reptile or amphibian touches its tongue to its Jacobson's organ.

Jacobson's organ

Tongue

244 Snakes have poor hearing and eyesight but they make up for it in other ways. They can find prey by picking up its vibrations travelling through the ground. Some snakes have pits in their faces that detect heat given off by prey. However, frogs and toads have good hearing.

243 Many reptiles and amphibians have an extra-special sense. They have something called a Jacobson's organ in the roof of their mouth, which they use to taste and smell the outside world.

Large ears detect sounds well

▶ Frogs and toads have large, well-developed eardrums just behind their eyes.

245 Geckos and iguanas have large eyes and good eyesight. They are a type of lizard that can't blink. Instead of having movable eyelids like humans, they have fixed, transparent 'spectacles' over their eyes. Most lizards have good sight – they need it to hunt down their small, fast insect prey.

246 One African gecko has extremely thin skin over its ear-openings. If you were to look at it with the openings lined up, you would see light coming through from the other side of its head!

Geckos lick their eyes to keep them clean

▲ Iguanas can see colour, and can smell and hear well.

Large eyes give the gecko excellent vision

◀ Nocturnal animals, like geckos, often have large eyes.

Feeling hungry

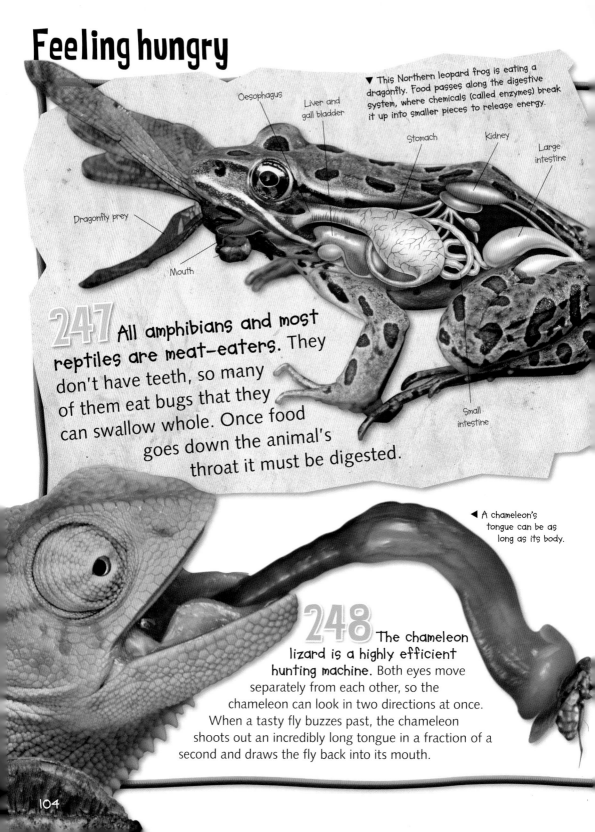

Oesophagus

Liver and gall bladder

▼ This Northern leopard frog is eating a dragonfly. Food passes along the digestive system, where chemicals (called enzymes) break it up into smaller pieces to release energy.

Stomach

Kidney

Large intestine

Dragonfly prey

Mouth

Small intestine

247 All amphibians and most reptiles are meat-eaters. They don't have teeth, so many of them eat bugs that they can swallow whole. Once food goes down the animal's throat it must be digested.

◀ A chameleon's tongue can be as long as its body.

248 The chameleon lizard is a highly efficient hunting machine. Both eyes move separately from each other, so the chameleon can look in two directions at once. When a tasty fly buzzes past, the chameleon shoots out an incredibly long tongue in a fraction of a second and draws the fly back into its mouth.

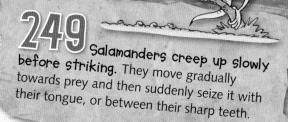

249 Salamanders creep up slowly before striking. They move gradually towards prey and then suddenly seize it with their tongue, or between their sharp teeth.

250 Large reptiles can manage massive meals! Crocodiles and big snakes open their jaws wide enough to bite animals that are as big as themselves. Crocodiles must bite lumps of meat off their prey to swallow, and they also swallow stones to help grind the food up.

◄ Crocodiles wait in shallow water for animals to come and drink, then leap up and drag their prey under the water.

BE A CHAMELEON

Like a chameleon, you need two eyes to judge distances easily. Close one eye, hold a finger out in front of you, and then try to touch this fingertip with the other. Now open both eyes and you'll find it a lot easier. Two eyes give your brain two slightly different angles to look at the object, so it is easier to tell how far away it is.

Fliers and leapers

251 Some reptiles and amphibians can take to the air – if only for a few seconds. This helps animals to travel further, escape predators or swoop down on passing prey before it gets away.

▼ A Blandford's flying lizard has thin wing-like flaps of skin that are supported by 5–7 pairs of ribs. It can travel up to 10 metres between trees.

253 Even certain kinds of snake can glide. The flying snake lives in the tropical forests of southern Asia. It can jump between branches or glide through the air in 'S' movements.

252 Reptiles that glide turn their bodies into parachutes. They are able to spread their bodies out, making them wide so they catch the air and slow their descent.

254 Flying geckos have wide, webbed feet. They use flaps of skin along their sides to help control their flight as they leap between trees. Flying geckos take to the air to avoid danger.

▼ The four webbed feet of a Wallace's flying frog help it to glide.

255 Some frogs can glide. Deep in the steamy rainforests of Southeast Asia and South America, tree frogs flit from tree to tree. Some can glide as far as 12 metres, clinging to their landing spot with suckers on their feet.

256 Frogs and toads use their powerful hind legs for hopping or jumping. The greatest frog leaper comes from Africa. Known as the rocket frog, it has been known to jump up to 4.2 metres.

① The powerful muscles in the frog's hind legs push off

② In mid-leap, the frog's hind legs are fully stretched out, its front legs are held back and its eyes are closed for protection

③ As it lands, its body arches and the front legs act as a brake

QUIZ

1. Where does the flying snake live?
2. How far can some tree frogs glide?
3. Which frog has been known to jump up to 4.2 metres?

Answers:
1. In the tropical forests of southern Asia 2. 12 metres 3. The rocket frog

Slitherers and crawlers

257 Most reptiles, and some amphibians, spend much of their time creeping, crawling and slithering along the ground. Scientists call the study of reptiles and amphibians 'herpetology', which comes from a Greek word meaning 'to creep or crawl'.

258 A snake's skin does not grow with its body. This means that it has to shed its skin to grow bigger. When a snake sheds its skin it is said to be moulting. Snakes moult at least once a year.

▲ Sidewinders have an unusual movement that allows them to slither over hot sand at speed.

▲ A moult begins at a snake's nose and can take up to 14 days to complete.

259 Some frogs and toads also shed their skin. The European toad sheds its skin several times during the summer – and then eats it! This recycles the goodness in the toad's skin.

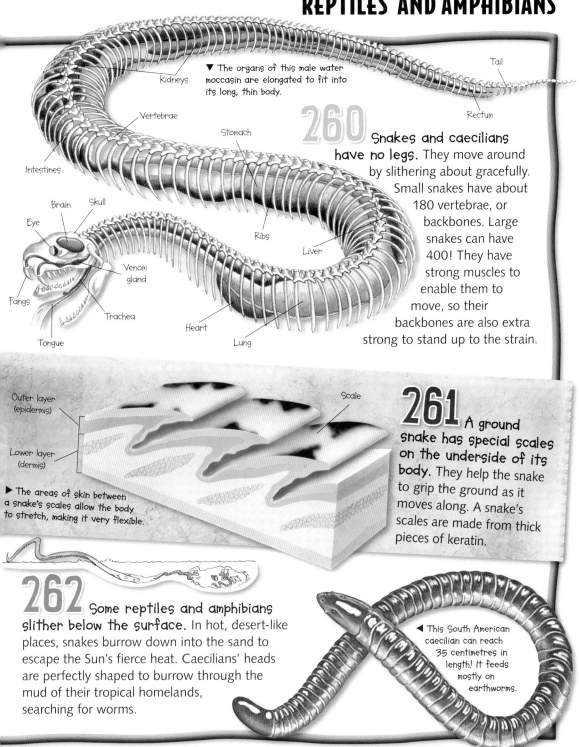

▼ The organs of this male water moccasin are elongated to fit into its long, thin body.

Kidneys

Tail

Vertebrae

Rectum

Stomach

260 **Snakes and caecilians have no legs.** They move around by slithering about gracefully. Small snakes have about 180 vertebrae, or backbones. Large snakes can have 400! They have strong muscles to enable them to move, so their backbones are also extra strong to stand up to the strain.

Intestines

Brain   Skull

Eye

Ribs

Liver

Venom gland

Fangs

Trachea

Heart

Lung

Tongue

Outer layer (epidermis)

Scale

Lower layer (dermis)

▶ The areas of skin between a snake's scales allow the body to stretch, making it very flexible.

261 **A ground snake has special scales on the underside of its body.** They help the snake to grip the ground as it moves along. A snake's scales are made from thick pieces of keratin.

262 **Some reptiles and amphibians slither below the surface.** In hot, desert-like places, snakes burrow down into the sand to escape the Sun's fierce heat. Caecilians' heads are perfectly shaped to burrow through the mud of their tropical homelands, searching for worms.

◀ This South American caecilian can reach 35 centimetres in length! It feeds mostly on earthworms.

Fast and slow

263 The reptile and amphibian worlds contain their fair share of fast and slow movers. However, a predator may be able to seize the slow-moving tortoise, but it will struggle to bite through its armour-plated shell!

264 Tortoises are among the slowest animals on Earth. The top speed for a giant tortoise is 5 metres a minute! These giant reptiles live on the Galapagos Islands in the Pacific Ocean and the Seychelles in the Indian Ocean.

265 Some lizards can run on water. Basilisks from Costa Rica and Philippine sail-fin water dragons leap into the water to escape from predators. They are good swimmers, but their most impressive trick is to sprint across the water's surface on their long hind legs.

◀ The enormous Galapagos giant tortoise may weigh as much as four adult humans.

FLAT RACE

Get a group of friends together and hold your own animal race day! Each of you cuts a flat animal shape – a frog or tortoise for example – out of paper or light card. Add details with coloured pencils or pens. Now race your animals along the ground to the finishing line by flapping a newspaper or a magazine behind them.

▼ A plumed basilisk uses its tail and wide feet to stay on the water's surface as it runs.

266 One of the world's slowest animals is the lizard-like tuatara. When resting, it breathes just once an hour, and may still be growing when it is 35 years old! Their slow lifestyle in part means that tuataras can live to be 120 years old.

▲ Tuataras live on a few small islands off the coast of New Zealand.

267 The fastest reptile in the world is the speedy spiny-tailed iguana. It can reach top speeds of 35 kilometres an hour. Racerunner lizards come a close second – in 1941 one of these racing reptiles ran at 29 kilometres an hour.

268 The fastest snake on land is the deadly black mamba. These shy African snakes are nervous reptiles that are easily scared – and quick to attack. This combination makes a mamba a snake to avoid!

Champion swimmers

269 Amphibians are well known for their links with water, but some types of reptile are also aquatic (live in or near water). Different types of amphibian and reptile have developed all kinds of ways of tackling watery lifestyles.

▼ Marine iguanas dive into chilly seawater to graze on seaweed. They can dive up to 9 metres at a time, but then have to bask to warm up again.

I DON'T BELIEVE IT!

Floating sea snakes can be surrounded by fish who gather at the snake's tail to avoid being eaten. When the snake fancies a snack, it swims backwards, fooling the fish into thinking its head is its tail!

270

Newts and salamanders swim rather like fish. They make an 'S' shape as they move. Many have flat tails that help to propel them through the water.

Eastern newt

▲▼ Newts are good swimmers and spend most of their lives in water.

Rough–skinned newt

271

Toads and frogs propel themselves by kicking back with their hind legs. They use their front legs as a brake for landing when they dive into the water. Large, webbed feet act like flippers, helping them to push through the water.

① Frog draws its legs up

③ The main kick back with toes spread propels the frog forward through the water

② It then pushes its feet out to the side

④ Frog closes its toes and draws its legs in and up for the next kick

272

A swimming snake may seem unlikely, but most snakes are experts in the water. Sea snakes can stay submerged for five hours and move rapidly through the water. European grass snakes are also good swimmers. They have to be because they eat animals that live around water.

▼ Sea snakes return to land to lay eggs.

▼ Green turtles took to the sea about 150 million years ago.

Yellow–bellied sea snake

273

Sea turtles have light, flat shells so they can move along more easily under water. Some have managed speeds of 29 kilometres an hour. Their flipper-like front legs 'fly' through the water. Their back legs form mini rudders for steering.

Banded sea snake

Nature's tanks

274 Tortoises and turtles are like armoured tanks – slow but well-protected by their shells. Tortoises live on land and eat mainly plants. Some turtles live in the salty sea, most of which are flesh-eaters. Other turtles, some of which are called terrapins, live in freshwater lakes and rivers.

◀ An eagle's huge talons grip onto a tortoise. The bird will fly with the tortoise, then drop it from a height to break its tough shell.

▶ A tortoise's shell is part of its body. It is attached to its skeleton.

275 When danger threatens, tortoises can quickly retreat into their mobile homes. They simply draw their head, tail and legs into their shell.

276 Tortoises and turtles are ancient members of the reptile world. They are the oldest living reptiles, and might have been around with the very first dinosaurs, about 200 million years ago. They also live longer than almost any other animal – some for up to 150 years!

Indian softshell turtle

Leopard tortoise

Matamata turtle

Hawksbill turtle

▲ Tortoises and turtles belong to a group of reptiles called Chelonians. They all have four limbs, a hard shell and a horny beak for a mouth. Their shells can be leathery or covered in plates.

277 Some sea turtles are among nature's greatest travellers. The green turtle migrates an amazing 2000 kilometres from its feeding grounds off the coast of Brazil to breeding sites such as Ascension Island, in the South Atlantic.

Dangerous enemies

278 Animals such as crocodiles, some snakes and snapping turtles make nasty enemies. Snakes are famed for poisoning or strangling prey before gobbling it down. Other reptiles have also found ways of making themselves especially dangerous.

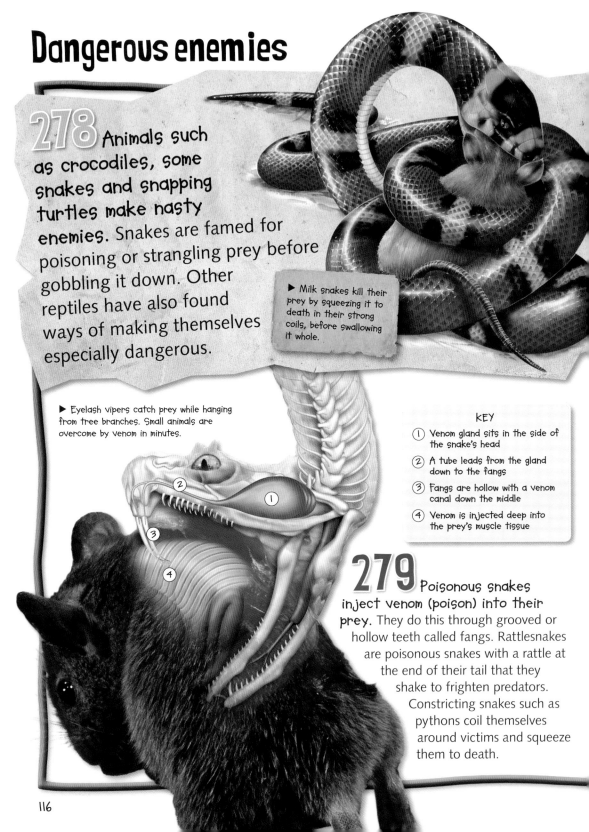

▶ Milk snakes kill their prey by squeezing it to death in their strong coils, before swallowing it whole.

▶ Eyelash vipers catch prey while hanging from tree branches. Small animals are overcome by venom in minutes.

KEY
① Venom gland sits in the side of the snake's head
② A tube leads from the gland down to the fangs
③ Fangs are hollow with a venom canal down the middle
④ Venom is injected deep into the prey's muscle tissue

279 Poisonous snakes inject venom (poison) into their prey. They do this through grooved or hollow teeth called fangs. Rattlesnakes are poisonous snakes with a rattle at the end of their tail that they shake to frighten predators. Constricting snakes such as pythons coil themselves around victims and squeeze them to death.

QUIZ

1. How does an alligator snapping turtle lure its prey?
2. How do poisonous snakes inject venom (poison) into their prey?
3. Which amphibian has bright yellow spots or stripes?

Answers:
1. By waving the tip of its tongue, which looks like a juicy worm 2. Through grooved or hollow teeth called fangs 3. A fire salamander

▼ Alligator snapping turtles can deliver one of the strongest bites in the animal world.

280 The alligator snapping turtle looks like a rough rock as it lies on the ocean floor. This cunning turtle has an extra trick up its sleeve. The tip of its tongue looks like a juicy worm, which it waves at passing prey to lure it into its jaws.

BEWARE! POISONOUS

► A fire salamander sprays foul poisons at a predator.

◄ The skin of a strawberry poison–dart frog is coated with deadly poison.

281 Bright patterns on some amphibians' skin warn predators. Their skin may be foul-tasting or cause irritation. Arrow-poison frogs from South America's rainforests have very bright colours, while fire salamanders have bright yellow spots or stripes.

Clever mimics

282 Reptiles and amphibians are masters of disguise. Some blend into their surroundings naturally, while others can change their appearance – perfect for avoiding predators or sneaking up on prey.

283 Frogs and toads are experts in the art of camouflage (blending with surroundings). Many are coloured shades of green or green-brown, to look just like leaves, grass or tree bark.

▶ A mossy frog's coloured and bumpy skin helps it blend into a tree trunk's mottled surface.

ANIMAL DISGUISE

Make a mask of your favourite reptile or amphibian from a round piece of card or a paper plate. Look at the pictures in this book to help you add details and colour it in. Carefully cut some eye holes, and then attach some string or elastic to the sides to hold it to your head.

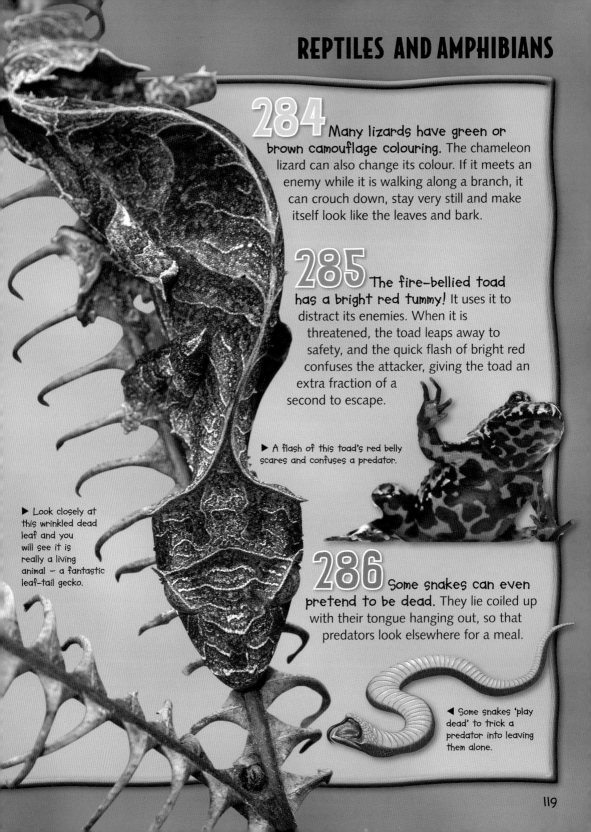

284 Many lizards have green or brown camouflage colouring. The chameleon lizard can also change its colour. If it meets an enemy while it is walking along a branch, it can crouch down, stay very still and make itself look like the leaves and bark.

285 The fire-bellied toad has a bright red tummy! It uses it to distract its enemies. When it is threatened, the toad leaps away to safety, and the quick flash of bright red confuses the attacker, giving the toad an extra fraction of a second to escape.

▶ A flash of this toad's red belly scares and confuses a predator.

▶ Look closely at this wrinkled dead leaf and you will see it is really a living animal – a fantastic leaf-tail gecko.

286 Some snakes can even pretend to be dead. They lie coiled up with their tongue hanging out, so that predators look elsewhere for a meal.

◀ Some snakes 'play dead' to trick a predator into leaving them alone.

Escape artists

287 Reptiles and amphibians must fight to survive in the deadly natural world. They might make a tasty meal for a predator, unless they have a clever trick or two. Gila monsters, for example, can deliver deadly bites packed with venom.

▶ A gila monster must bite and chew to release its venom.

288 Some salamanders and lizards have detachable tails. If a predator grabs a five-lined tree skink lizard by the tail, it will be left holding a twitching blue tail! The tail does grow back.

289 Spraying an attacker with blood is a good trick. Desert horned lizards puff themselves up, hiss and squirt blood out of their eyes when they are scared.

◀ A desert horned lizard's bloody face is fearsome.

▶ A skink could make a juicy snack for a bigger animal.

QUIZ

1. What do some salamanders and lizards have to help them escape predators?
2. What do desert horned lizards do when they are scared?
3. What is a rattlesnake's rattle formed of?

Answers:
1. Detachable tails
2. Puff themselves up, hiss and squirt blood out of their eyes
3. Layers of dried, moulted skin

290 A young blue-tongued skink uses colour as a delay tactic. The lizard simply flashes its bright blue tongue and mouth lining at an enemy. The startled predator lets its prey slip away.

▼ Can you tell which end is the shingleback lizard's head?

291 The Australian shingleback lizard has a tail shaped like a head. By the time a confused predator has worked this one out, the lizard has made its getaway.

292 Rattlesnakes are dangerous reptiles. They shake the rattles on their tails to warn attackers before they strike. Their long fangs pump deadly venom deep into the flesh.

◀ A rattlesnake's rattle is formed of layers of dried, moulted skin.

Mega reptiles

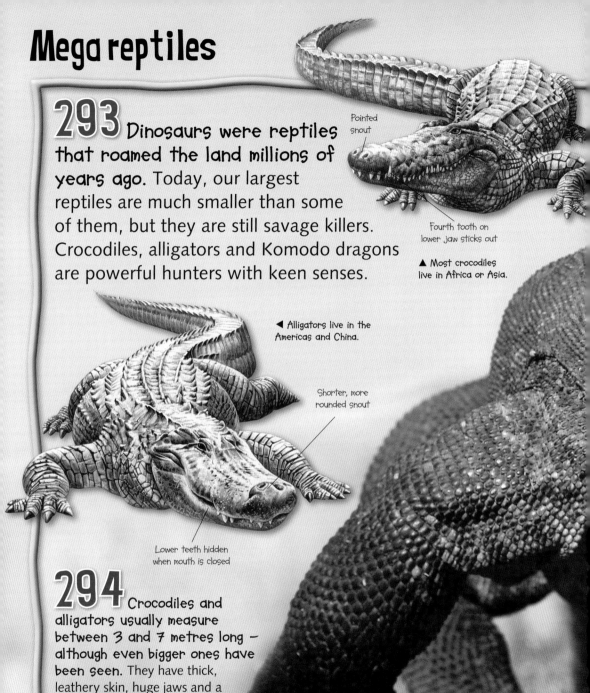

293 Dinosaurs were reptiles that roamed the land millions of years ago. Today, our largest reptiles are much smaller than some of them, but they are still savage killers. Crocodiles, alligators and Komodo dragons are powerful hunters with keen senses.

Pointed snout

Fourth tooth on lower jaw sticks out

▲ Most crocodiles live in Africa or Asia.

◀ Alligators live in the Americas and China.

Shorter, more rounded snout

Lower teeth hidden when mouth is closed

294 Crocodiles and alligators usually measure between 3 and 7 metres long — although even bigger ones have been seen. They have thick, leathery skin, huge jaws and a killer instinct. Crocodiles have two big teeth on their lower jaws that can be seen even when their mouth is shut.

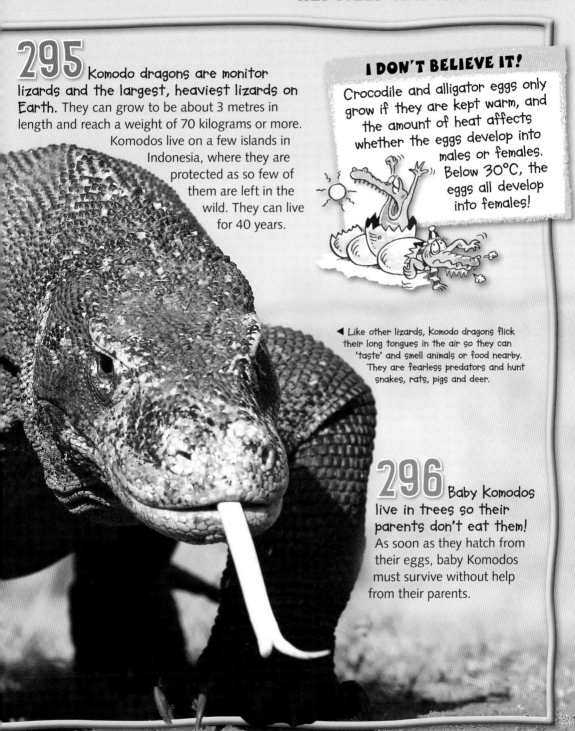

295 Komodo dragons are monitor lizards and the largest, heaviest lizards on Earth. They can grow to be about 3 metres in length and reach a weight of 70 kilograms or more. Komodos live on a few islands in Indonesia, where they are protected as so few of them are left in the wild. They can live for 40 years.

I DON'T BELIEVE IT!

Crocodile and alligator eggs only grow if they are kept warm, and the amount of heat affects whether the eggs develop into males or females. Below 30°C, the eggs all develop into females!

◀ Like other lizards, Komodo dragons flick their long tongues in the air so they can 'taste' and smell animals or food nearby. They are fearless predators and hunt snakes, rats, pigs and deer.

296 Baby Komodos live in trees so their parents don't eat them! As soon as they hatch from their eggs, baby Komodos must survive without help from their parents.

Reptiles in danger

297 One-third of all reptiles and amphibians are at risk of dying out forever. They are at risk of extinction because they are losing their habitats (homes) or because they have been hunted.

298 Green turtles may die out because people steal their eggs to sell as food. Their breeding beaches have also been taken over by hotels or houses, or ruined with pollution. Adult green turtles are captured in the seas around Asia and then eaten.

▶ Scientists hope to save green turtles from extinction. They tag them and follow their movements across the oceans.

REPTILES AND AMPHIBIANS

Cecchelone abingdoni
RIP
24 de Junio 2012 / June 24th 2012

Solitario George   Lonesome George

Prometemos contar tu historia   We promise to tell your story
transmitir tu mensaje de conservación   and to share your conservation message

▲ Lonesome George's death has inspired many people to save the last giant tortoises.

299 Lonesome George was a type of giant tortoise and the last of his kind. He lived on the Galapagos Islands, where turtles were once common reptiles. When he died in 2012, George's sub-species became extinct forever.

300 Amphibians are at risk from climate change. They need their homes to stay warm and damp, but pollution is changing our planet's weather systems. Many frogs and toads have also died from a skin disease that has spread around the world.

▲ Panamanian golden frogs are probably extinct in the wild.

QUIZ

1. In what year did Lonesome George die?
2. How are scientists trying to save green turtles from extinction?
3. Which frogs are probably extinct in the wild?

Answers:
1. 2012 2. By tagging them and following their movements across the oceans 3. Panamanian golden frogs

125

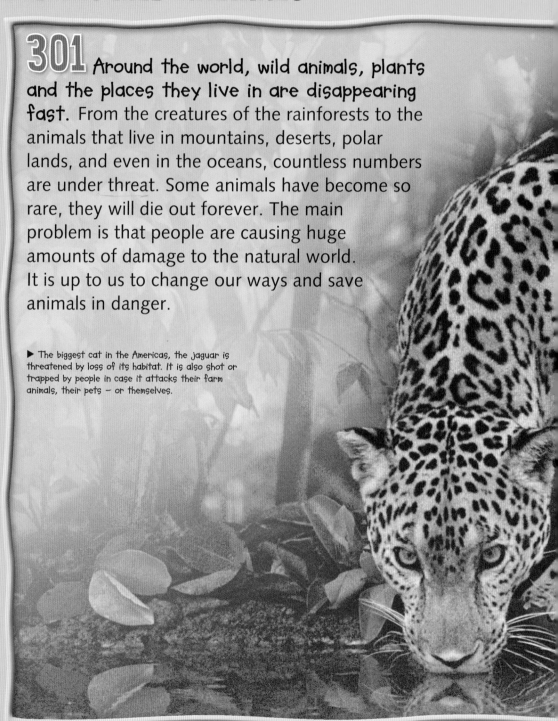

ENDANGERED ANIMALS

301 Around the world, wild animals, plants and the places they live in are disappearing fast. From the creatures of the rainforests to the animals that live in mountains, deserts, polar lands, and even in the oceans, countless numbers are under threat. Some animals have become so rare, they will die out forever. The main problem is that people are causing huge amounts of damage to the natural world. It is up to us to change our ways and save animals in danger.

▶ The biggest cat in the Americas, the jaguar is threatened by loss of its habitat. It is also shot or trapped by people in case it attacks their farm animals, their pets — or themselves.

Too late to save

302 In the last few hundred years, many kinds of animals have become endangered, and dozens have died out. They include fish, frogs, snakes, birds and mammals. Studying why these extinctions happened can help to save today's endangered animals.

303 Being very common is no safeguard against human threats. Five hundred years ago there were perhaps 5000 million passenger pigeons. They were shot and trapped by people for their meat, and their natural habitats were taken over by crops and farm animals. The last passenger pigeon, 'Martha', died in Cincinnati Zoo in 1914.

304 A creature that went from discovery to extinction in less than 30 years was Steller's sea cow. It was a huge, 3-tonne cousin of the manatee and dugong, and lived in the Arctic region. It was first described by scientists in 1741. So many were killed in a short space of time that Steller's sea cow had died out by 1768.

QUIZ

What died out when? Put these animals' extinctions in order, from most long ago to most recent.

A. Dodo
B. Blue antelope
C. Thylacine
D. Passenger pigeon
E. Steller's sea cow

Answers:
A E B D C

128

▶ The dodo has become a world symbol of extinction. Only a few bones, feathers and bits of skin remain.

▲ Steller's sea cow was 8 metres long and almost as heavy as an elephant. However size was no protection, as its herds were slaughtered by sailors for meat, blubber and hides.

306 The dodo, a turkey-sized bird with tiny wings that could not fly, was found on the island of Mauritius in the Indian Ocean. Sailors that stopped at the island captured dodos as fresh food. So many were killed that all dodos were extinct by 1700. This has led to the saying 'as dead as a dodo'.

305 Many animals have become endangered, and died out forever. They include the blue antelope of Southern Africa (around 1800), the flightless seabird known as the great auk (1850s), the dog-like marsupial (pouched mammal) known as the thylacine or Tasmanian tiger (1936), and the Caribbean monk seal (1950s). The list is very long, and very sad.

▶ Every 7 September, Australia holds National Threatened Species Day. The day is in memory of the last thylacine that died on this date in 1936 at Hobart Zoo, in the state of Tasmania.

How we know

307 How do we know which animals are endangered and need our help? Explorers and travellers bring back stories of rare and strange creatures. Sometimes they add bits to their tales to make them more exciting. Scientific studies and surveys are needed to find out which creatures are in trouble, and how serious the threats are.

▼ This lion, put to sleep briefly by a tranquillizer dart, is being tracked by its radio collar. Each lion has its own pattern of whisker spots, like a fingerprint, to help identify it.

▼ Rangers guard incredibly rare mountain gorillas, which soon get used to having them around. The rangers become well acquainted with the habits of the gorillas, which helps scientists carry out important research.

308 Firing a dart containing a knock-out chemical makes a creature, such as a lion, sleep for a short time. Scientists then work fast to take blood samples, check for diseases, measure and weigh, and gather other useful information, before the animal wakes up.

309 Scientists need to know more than just how many individual animals are left in an endangered species. They try to find out the animals' ages, what they eat, how often they breed, how they move about or migrate, and how long they live. This all helps to build up knowledge of the species, and work out the best ways to take action.

▼ Aerial films and photographs can be studied to count big animals such as elephants, estimate their age and work out if they are male or female.

310 Big animals in open habitats, such as elephants on the African savanna (grassland), are surveyed from the air. Planes, helicopters and even balloons carry people who count the herds and take photographs.

I DON'T BELIEVE IT!

When studying an endangered animal, one of the best things to have is — its poo! Droppings or dung contain much information about what a creature eats, how healthy it is, and any diseases it may have.

311 It is extremely helpful to capture, tag and release animals. Rare birds such as albatrosses are carefully caught in nets, and small rings are put on their legs. This helps scientists to identify each albatross every time it is seen. Tags in the ears of rhinos can work in the same way.

312 Some animals are big enough to attach a radio beacon to, which sends signals up to a satellite. Whales, sea turtles, seals and other sea creatures can be tracked as they swim across the vast oceans.

How endangered?

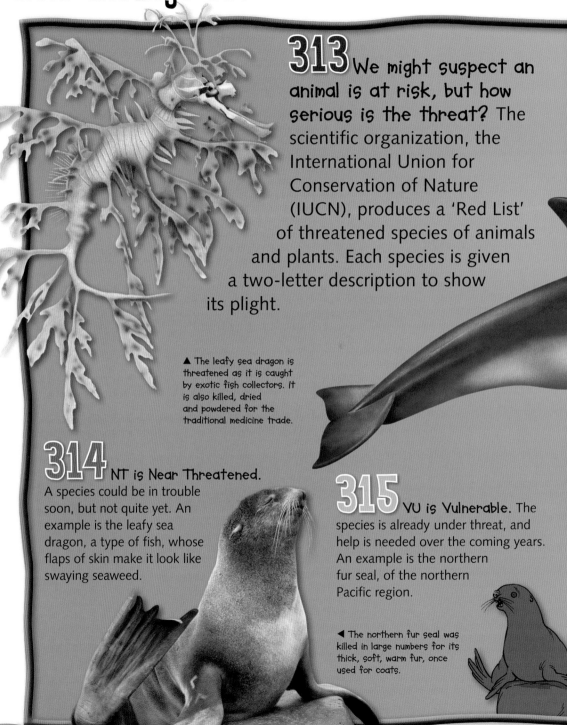

313 We might suspect an animal is at risk, but how serious is the threat? The scientific organization, the International Union for Conservation of Nature (IUCN), produces a 'Red List' of threatened species of animals and plants. Each species is given a two-letter description to show its plight.

▲ The leafy sea dragon is threatened as it is caught by exotic fish collectors. It is also killed, dried and powdered for the traditional medicine trade.

314 NT is Near Threatened. A species could be in trouble soon, but not quite yet. An example is the leafy sea dragon, a type of fish, whose flaps of skin make it look like swaying seaweed.

315 VU is Vulnerable. The species is already under threat, and help is needed over the coming years. An example is the northern fur seal, of the northern Pacific region.

◄ The northern fur seal was killed in large numbers for its thick, soft, warm fur, once used for coats.

▶ Snow leopards are found in the remote mountains of central Asia. Hunting by humans has driven them out of many areas.

316 EN is Endangered.
The species faces big problems and the risk of extinction over the coming years is high. An example is the beautiful snow leopard.

317 CR is Critically Endangered.
This is the most serious group. Unless there is a huge conservation effort, extinction is just around the corner. An example is the vaquita, the smallest kind of porpoise, from the northern Gulf of California.

▲ Polluted water, drilling for oil and gas, and being caught in fishing nets are all deadly dangers for the 1.5-metre-long vaquita.

▼ Hawaiian crows are only found in captivity. Attempts to breed and release them have so far failed.

318 EW is Extinct in the Wild.
The species has disappeared in nature, although there may be a few surviving in zoos and wildlife parks. An example is the Hawaiian crow. The last two wild birds disappeared in 2002, although some live in cages. EX is Extinct, or gone forever. Usually this means the animal has not been seen for 50 years.

MATCH UP
Can you place these threatened creatures in their correct animal groups?

A. Whale shark   1. Bird
B. Spix macaw   2. Fish
C. Vaquita   3. Amphibian
D. Caiman   4. Mammal
E. Olm   5. Reptile

Answers:
A2 B1 C4 D5 E3

On the critical list

319 The most threatened animals in the world are CR, Critically Endangered. One of the most famous CR mammals is the mountain gorilla. There are just a few hundred left in the high peaks of Central Africa. They suffer from loss of their natural habitat, being killed for meat and trophies, and from catching human diseases.

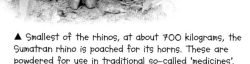

▲ Smallest of the rhinos, at about 700 kilograms, the Sumatran rhino is poached for its horns. These are powdered for use in traditional so-called 'medicines'.

320 The most threatened group of big mammals is the rhinos. Of the five species, three are CR – the Javan and Sumatran rhinos of Southeast Asia, and the black rhino of Africa. The Indian rhino is vulnerable, VU. They all suffer from loss of natural living areas and being killed for their horns.

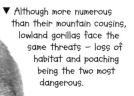

▼ Although more numerous than their mountain cousins, lowland gorillas face the same threats – loss of habitat and poaching being the two most dangerous.

MAKE A RHINO NOSE

You will need:
large sheet of card   sticky tape

A rhino's nose horn may be more than one metre long! Make your own by rolling some card into a cone shape and taping it firmly. Hold the 'horn' angled up from your own nose. How do rhinos see where they are going?

321
The kouprey or Cambodian forest ox is another critical mammal. It has big horns and weighs more than one tonne, but there are probably fewer than 250 left in Southeast Asia. Apart from losing its natural habitat, the kouprey is hunted by local people and it catches diseases from farm cattle. It is also killed for food by soldiers who fight for local warlords and hide in the forest.

▲ The kouprey grazes on grasses by night and hides in the thick forest during the day.

▼ Right whales are slow swimmers and stay near the surface, which made them easy targets for whalers.

322
The northern right whale has never recovered from being slaughtered during the mass killing of whales in the last century. There are now probably less than 600 left. These whales breed so slowly that they may never increase in numbers.

323
Apart from big, well-known mammals, many other smaller mammal species are on the critical list. They include the Mexican agouti (a type of rodent), the riverine rabbit of South Africa and the northern hairy-nosed wombat of northeast Australia.

All kinds under threat

324 Mammals such as gorillas, whales and tigers are not the only endangered animals – there are many other threatened species from all animal groups. Among the birds is the Bermuda petrel, the national seabird of the island of Bermuda. Only about 250 survive and the islanders are making a huge conservation effort to help them.

▲ The young Bermuda petrel stays at sea for about five years before it comes back to land to breed.

325 A critical reptile is the Batagur baska (river turtle or terrapin) of India and Southeast Asia. One reason for its rarity was that people collected its eggs, especially in Cambodia, to give as presents to the king. King Norodom Sihamoni of Cambodia has now given orders to protect the baska.

▼ The batagur 'royal turtle' grows to more than one metre long and 30 kilograms in weight. It eats all kinds of foods, from plants to fish and crabs.

326 A vulnerable amphibian is Hamilton's frog of New Zealand. It is perhaps the rarest frog in the world. Hamilton's frog does not croak, does not have webbed feet, and hatches from its egg not as a tadpole, but as a fully formed froglet.

▲ Hamilton's frog is less than 5 cm long. There may be as few as 300 left in the wild.

▼ The Devil's Hole pupfish is one of several very rare fish, each found in one small pool.

327 A fish that is critically endangered is the Devil's Hole pupfish. It lives naturally in just one warm pool, Devil's Hole, in a limestone cave in the desert near Death Valley, USA. There were around 200–400 pupfish there, but after problems with floods and droughts, the number is currently less than 100.

328 One of the rarest insects is the Queen Alexandra's birdwing butterfly. It lives in a small area on the island of Papua New Guinea. In 1950, a nearby volcano erupted and destroyed much of the butterfly's forest habitat, so it is now endangered (EN).

▶ Like many tropical butterflies, the female and male Queen Alexandra's birdwing look quite different from each other.

Male

Female

137

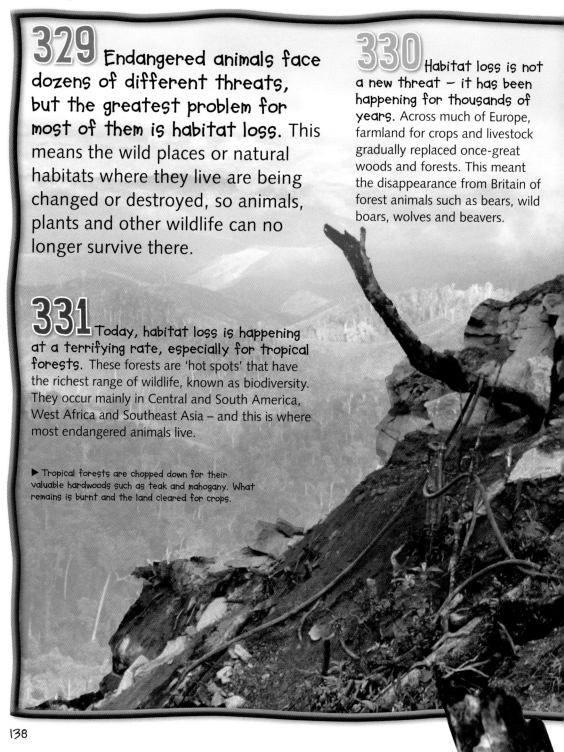

The greatest threat

329 Endangered animals face dozens of different threats, but the greatest problem for most of them is habitat loss. This means the wild places or natural habitats where they live are being changed or destroyed, so animals, plants and other wildlife can no longer survive there.

330 Habitat loss is not a new threat – it has been happening for thousands of years. Across much of Europe, farmland for crops and livestock gradually replaced once-great woods and forests. This meant the disappearance from Britain of forest animals such as bears, wild boars, wolves and beavers.

331 Today, habitat loss is happening at a terrifying rate, especially for tropical forests. These forests are 'hot spots' that have the richest range of wildlife, known as biodiversity. They occur mainly in Central and South America, West Africa and Southeast Asia – and this is where most endangered animals live.

▶ Tropical forests are chopped down for their valuable hardwoods such as teak and mahogany. What remains is burnt and the land cleared for crops.

332 The muriquis or woolly spider monkeys of Brazil are critically endangered. Trees in their tropical forests have been chopped down for logs and the timber trade. Then the land is cleared for farm animals and crops. The monkeys, along with thousands of other forest species, have much smaller areas in which to live.

333 In Borneo, animals from pygmy elephants to orang-utans are under threat as their forests are cleared for oil palm trees and other crops. Oil palm plantations are one of the main reasons for habitat loss across the tropics. The vegetable oil from the fleshy fruits is used for cooking, to make margarine and prepared meals, and for a vehicle fuel known as biodiesel.

Too many people

334 Many animals no longer live in their natural habitats because people now live there. The number of people in the world increases by about 150 every minute. They need houses, land for farms, shops, schools, factories and roads. More people means fewer places for wildlife.

335 Animals living in lakes, rivers, marshes and swamps are some of the most endangered. Their habitats are drained and cleared for towns, ports and waterside holiday centres. Tourist areas along rivers and coastlines endanger all kinds of animals.

▼ Across the world, cities spread into nearby natural habitats, such as this shanty town in Colombia, South America.

QUIZ

Can you name the major threats these animals face?

1. Mediterranean monk seal
2. Red panda
3. Black-necked crane
4. Golden bamboo lemur

Answers:
1. Spread of holiday areas along the Mediterranean 2. Loss of bamboo 3. Tourists 4. Loss of trees in Madagascar due to spreading villages and farms

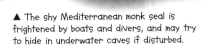

336
The Mediterranean monk seal has suffered greatly from the spread of tourism. Its breeding and resting areas have been taken over for holiday villages, sunbathing beaches and water sports. This seal has also been affected by pollution and hunted by fisherman, who believe it 'steals' their fish. It is now endangered, with fewer than 600 left.

▲ The shy Mediterranean monk seal is frightened by boats and divers, and may try to hide in underwater caves if disturbed.

337
The black-necked crane lives in the highlands around the Himalayas in Asia. It faces several threats. One is the development of tourism in a region known as the Ladakh Valley in India. People come to gaze at the marvellous scenery and watch the wildlife, but they disturb the cranes, who are shy and less likely to breed.

▶ Black-necked cranes are sometimes poisoned by pesticide chemicals used by farmers.

338
The giant panda is a famous rare animal, and its distant cousin, the red panda, is also under threat. This tree-dwelling bamboo-eater from South and East Asia has fewer places to live, as towns and villages spread quickly. It's also hunted for its fur, especially its bushy tail, which is used to make hats and good luck wedding charms.

▶ The red panda is fully protected by law, but hunting continues for its fur.

Pollution problems

339 Pollution is a threat to all wildlife, as the wastes and chemicals we make get into the air, soil and water. Like many dangers to animals, pollution is often combined with other threats, such as habitat loss and climate change. Sometimes it is difficult to separate these dangers, since one is part of another.

▲ This Atlantic croaker fish has become blind with misty eyes, or cataracts, due to chemicals in the water.

340 Harmful chemicals spread quickly through water to affect streams, rivers, lakes and even the open ocean. Caspian seals live in the landlocked Caspian Sea, a vast lake in West Asia. Industries and factories around the lake shore pollute its waters. The seals suffer from sores and fur loss, and are less resistant to diseases.

◄ Oil spillages are a devastating form of pollution. This bird is covered in oil, which waterlogs its feathers. The bird is also in danger of being poisoned by swallowing oil as it tries to clean itself.

341 The largest amphibians in the world are Chinese and Japanese giant salamanders. They are in danger from pollution of their cool, fast-flowing, highland streams. There are few factories there, but the clouds and rains carry polluting chemicals from the smoke and fumes of factory chimneys far away.

POLLUTION HAZARDS

Next time you are in the park or countryside, look out for types of pollution. Find out how they could harm animals, and how we can reduce them. Look for examples such as:

Litter in ponds • Plastic bags in bushes and hedges • Pools of oil or fuel from vehicles Broken glass • Pipes carrying poisonous liquids into ditches, streams or rivers • Metal wire, plastic tags and similar objects

▼ The baiji's home in the Yangtze River has become a dangerous, polluted place. The last sighting of one of these dolphins was in 2004.

342 A survey in 2006 failed to find any baijis, or Chinese river dolphins. One of the threats to this dolphin is pollution of its main river, the Yangtze or Chang Jiang, by factories along its banks, and by farm chemicals seeping into the water from fields. The pollution has harmed not only the baiji but also the fish and other animals that it eats. Further threats include hunting by people for its meat, the building of dams, drowning in fishing nets and being hit by boats.

Baiji (Chinese river dolphin)

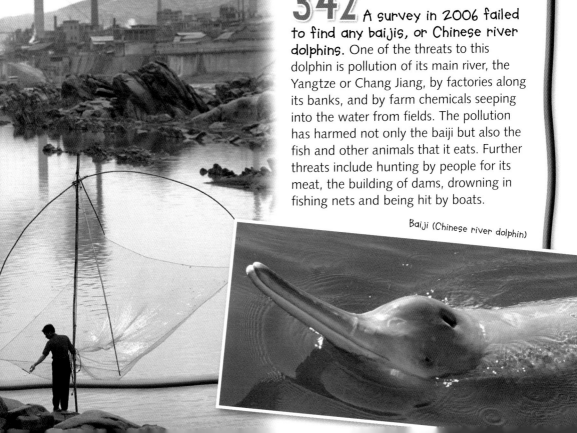

A change in the weather

343 The whole world faces climate change, which could endanger many animal species. The weather is gradually becoming warmer because our atmosphere (the layer of air around Earth) is being altered by 'greenhouse gases'. These come mainly from burning fuels such as petrol, diesel, wood, coal and natural gas. They make the Earth trap heat from the Sun, and so the planet gets hotter.

▲ Penguins become tired after feeding in the water for several hours, and need to rest on the shore or an iceberg. Global warming means that the ice is melting and penguins' resting places are disappearing.

344 In the far north, polar bears are threatened because ice floes (big lumps of ice) are melting faster. The bears use the ice floes to hunt seals from and to rest on. There used to be plenty of floes, but now polar bears can swim for hours before finding one. Some bears even drown, exhausted in the open sea.

345 In the far south, penguins have trouble finding icebergs to rest on. As in the north, the icebergs melt faster due to global warming. Like the polar bears, the penguins cannot get out of the water for a rest, and because they cannot fly, they may drown.

▶ Fewer, smaller ice floes spell terrible trouble for polar bears.

346
Global warming is changing the seasons, which may affect huge numbers of animals. An earlier spring means that insects in Europe breed a week or two before they used to. However, migrating birds from Africa, such as pied flycatchers, swallows and swifts, might arrive too late to catch the insects for their chicks. Scientists call this 'uncoupling' of the natural links between animals and their seasonal food.

347
The huge Asian fish, the beluga sturgeon, is already critically endangered. It is poached for the female's eggs, which are sold as the expensive food caviar. However, as global warming continues, the sturgeon's rivers and lakes will be affected, which could push the fish to extinction even more quickly.

I DON'T BELIEVE IT!
Scientists studying 40,000 tree swallows say that the birds now lay their eggs nine days earlier than they did 40 years ago, probably as a result of global warming.

▲ Beluga sturgeons used to grow to more than 5 metres long, but most of them are now caught and killed before they reach such a great size.

Poaching and souvenirs

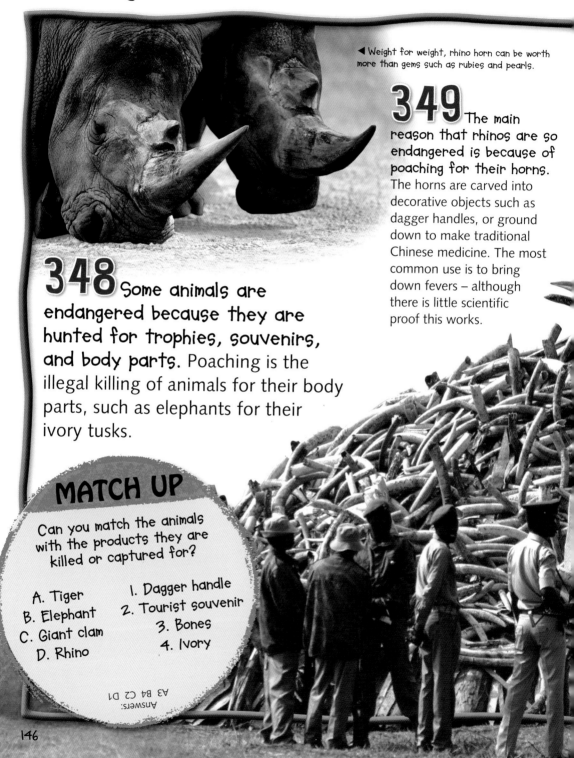

◀ Weight for weight, rhino horn can be worth more than gems such as rubies and pearls.

349 The main reason that rhinos are so endangered is because of poaching for their horns. The horns are carved into decorative objects such as dagger handles, or ground down to make traditional Chinese medicine. The most common use is to bring down fevers – although there is little scientific proof this works.

348 Some animals are endangered because they are hunted for trophies, souvenirs, and body parts. Poaching is the illegal killing of animals for their body parts, such as elephants for their ivory tusks.

MATCH UP

Can you match the animals with the products they are killed or captured for?

A. Tiger
B. Elephant
C. Giant clam
D. Rhino

1. Dagger handle
2. Tourist souvenir
3. Bones
4. Ivory

Answers:
A3 B4 C2 D1

350 Rhinos are not the only victims of traditional medicines. In parts of Asia and South America, tiger bones are ground into powders for making pills, blood from sea turtles is drunk fresh, and horns of rare antelopes and gazelles are mashed into soup.

▼ This bonfire of seized elephant ivory was built in Kenya in 1989. Huge piles of tusks were burnt to try and stop the trade in ivory, but it did not succeed.

351 On holiday, some people buy souvenirs — some of which are made from endangered animals. The souvenir trade threatens shellfish such as conches and giant clams, starfish, sea urchins, and unusual fish such as seahorses. People can buy items carved from the ivory of elephants and walruses, deer antlers and antelope horns. People should avoid all animal souvenirs (and rare plants too).

352 The trade in animal body parts and products is controlled by national and international rules. Most countries have signed the agreement called CITES, the Convention on International Trade in Endangered Species. However, in thick jungles and remote places, it's difficult to stop poaching, while smugglers always invent new tricks to get illegal items from place to place.

▶ Buying tourist souvenirs such as dried seahorses simply supports the catching and killing of them.

Island problems

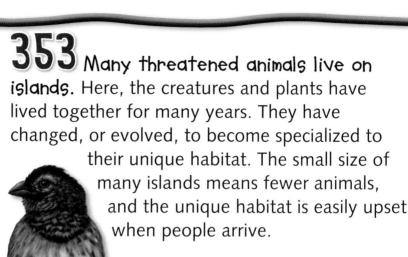

353 **Many threatened animals live on islands.** Here, the creatures and plants have lived together for many years. They have changed, or evolved, to become specialized to their unique habitat. The small size of many islands means fewer animals, and the unique habitat is easily upset when people arrive.

Mangrove finch

▲ Each type of Galapagos Island finch, including this mangrove finch, has evolved a beak shape suited to eating certain kinds of food.

354 **The mangrove finch, which lives on the Galapagos Islands in the Pacific Ocean, is critically endangered.** It is one of Darwin's finches – the birds that helped English naturalist Charles Darwin (1809–1882) work out his theory of evolution, which is so important to science.

355 **Also on the Galapagos, giant tortoises are under threat, partly due to a common island problem – introduced species.** People have taken many animals to islands, such as cats, rats, rabbits and dogs. These new arrivals destroy the natural habitat, prey on some local species, and compete for food and shelter.

▶ Volcan Alcedo tortoises are the largest group of giant tortoises in the Galapagos, although they are listed as vulnerable, VU.

I DON'T BELIEVE IT!

On the island of Cuba, the rare, shrew-like Cuban solenodon or almiqui, was thought to be extinct. One was caught alive in 2003. Named Alejandrito, he became a celebrity, was studied for two days, and released unharmed.

356 **The island of Madagascar has amazing and unique wildlife, but much of it is in danger.** Lemurs, such as the ring-tailed lemur, are found nowhere else in the wild. However, many Madagascan species are threatened by a mixture of habitat loss, hunting for food, capture for the illegal pet trade, and the problem of introduced species.

◀ Ring-tailed lemurs are popular in wildlife parks and zoos, but are becoming rarer on their island home of Madagascar.

357 **There have been more than 700 known animal extinctions in the last 400 years – and about half of these were on islands.** In the Hawaiian islands alone about 25 kinds of birds, 70 types of snails, 80 kinds of insects and more than 100 types of plants have disappeared in the past 200 years.

358 **On islands, not just exciting species such as giant tortoises and colourful birds are threatened.** There are less glamorous species, such as the partula snails of the South Pacific islands. They were eaten by a predatory snail called Euglandina, which was introduced to provide food for local people.

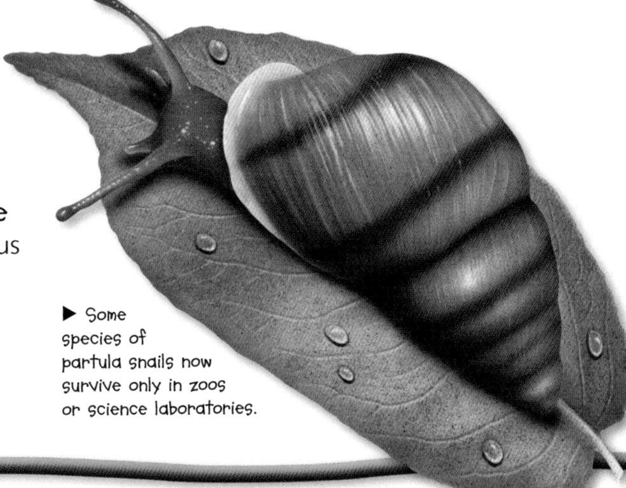

▶ Some species of partula snails now survive only in zoos or science laboratories.

Stop the slaughter

359 For more than 50 years there has been a growing awareness of endangered animals and how we can save them. 'Headline' species such as whales, tigers, orang-utans and gorillas grab the interest of people and help to raise money for conservation. This conservation work can then protect natural habitats and so save many other species as well.

▲ The Born Free Foundation is an international wildlife charity working around the world to protect threatened species in the wild.

360 In the 1960s, the giant panda of China became famous as the symbol of the World Wildlife Fund, also known as the World Wide Fund for Nature (WWF). Huge conservation efforts mean the giant panda is now off the critical list, with some 2000 in the wild, although it is still listed as VU, vulnerable.

◄ Pandas eat almost nothing but particular kinds of bamboo, so they rely heavily on their specialized habitat.

I DON'T BELIEVE IT!

The giant panda was chosen as a symbol of conservation partly because of its black–and–white colours. These make its image easier to photocopy without the need for any colours.

361 In the 1970s, people started to protest against the commercial hunting of great whales, which was threatening many species. 'Save the Whale' campaigns and marches became popular. Eventually in 1980 there was a world ban on the mass hunting of large whales.

362 In the 1980s, there were many anti-fur campaigns, to stop the killing of wild cats and other animals for their fur coats. This helped to reduce one of the threats to many beautiful cat species, not only big cats, but also medium and small species such as the ocelot and margay. Sadly, fur is becoming a popular fashion item once more.

363 In the 1990s, the terrible crisis facing the tiger became clear. Save the Tiger Fund was founded in 1995 to fight the many dangers facing the biggest of big cats. However, it is too late for some varieties, or subspecies, of tiger. The Balinese tiger from the island of Bali became extinct in the 1930s, and the Javan tiger followed in the 1980s.

▶ Great whales, such as these blue whales, are now fairly safe from mass slaughter. However, they breed very slowly and their numbers will take many years to start rising again.

A place to live

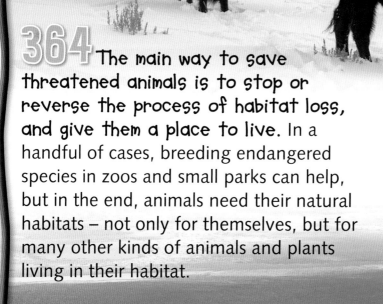

364 The main way to save threatened animals is to stop or reverse the process of habitat loss, and give them a place to live. In a handful of cases, breeding endangered species in zoos and small parks can help, but in the end, animals need their natural habitats – not only for themselves, but for many other kinds of animals and plants living in their habitat.

▲ Bison were just saved from extinction and now roam freely in Yellowstone, Wood Buffalo and other North American parks.

▼ The Great Barrier Reef Marine Park has gradually been extended over the years, with limited tourism in some areas and complete protection in others.

365 Natural places are preserved by setting aside large areas as national parks, nature reserves and wildlife sanctuaries. In 1872, Yellowstone National Park in the USA became the world's first national park. As in other protected areas, there are laws preventing people from damaging the animals, plants or habitat. Yellowstone's animals include the American bison or 'buffalo', which used to roam the prairies in millions. It almost became extinct in the 1880s but was just saved.

366 Some of the most important and precious wild areas are given the title of World Heritage Site. In Ethiopia, East Africa, the Simien National Park is home to extremely rare animals such as the gelada baboon, the Ethiopian wolf (Simien fox or jackal), and a type of wild goat called the Walia ibex, of which there are only 500 left.

▲ The 500 surviving Ethiopian wolves are found in only a few areas, such as the Bale Mountains and Simien National Park in Ethiopia.

367 One of the world's biggest protected ocean areas is Australia's Great Barrier Reef Marine Park. It is home to a vast array of amazing animals from tiny coral creatures, to green turtles, to huge sharks. In 2006 the US set up the even bigger NorthWest Hawaiian Island National Monument. This reserve is home to more than 7000 animal species including the threatened Hawaiian monk seal and the Laysan albatross.

QUIZ

Where would you find these rare animals?
1. Ethiopian wolf
2. American bison
3. Hawaiian monk seal
4. Green turtle

Answers:
1. Simien National Park, Ethiopia 2. Yellowstone National Park, USA 3. NorthWest Hawaiian Island National Monument 4. Great Barrier Reef, Australia

Captive breeding

368 Zoos, wildlife parks and breeding centres may play an important role in saving animals. Some animals are kept and encouraged to breed and build up their numbers, hopefully for release back into the wild. This method needs expert knowledge about the species, so the zoo keepers can look after the animals well. However, it can only be used in selected cases.

369 Not only big exciting animals are bred in captivity — one of the smallest is the Chatham Island black robin. By the early 1980s, only five remained, with just one female, 'Old Blue'. Careful captive breeding involved taking away her first batch of eggs, so she would lay a second clutch, while keepers cared for the first batch so they hatched. There are now more than 250 black robins.

▼ When rare animals such as the giant panda are reared in captivity, scientists can learn much about them.

◀ The captive population of Pere David's deer is increasing.

I DON'T BELIEVE IT!

In 1986, there were only about 50 black–footed ferrets left, all in Wyoming, USA. After 20 years of captive breeding and release, there are now more than 600 in the wild.

370 For many years, Pere David's deer lived only in reserves owned by the emperors of China. Gradually the deer disappeared – many were eaten. However, a few were taken to Woburn animal park in the UK, where they bred. In the 1980s, some Pere David's deer were reintroduced into a nature reserve in China. They are still EW, extinct in the wild.

▼ Blue Iguanas are tagged so they can be closely monitored in their protected areas.

371 The endangered Grand Cayman Blue Iguana was down to fewer than 15 lizards. Since 1996, captive-bred lizards have been released into protected areas on the island of Grand Cayman, and more reserves and releases are planned.

▼ Tigers breed well in some zoos, but release into the wild is virtually impossible. Captive tigers lose their instinct to kill, so may starve to death.

372 There are many problems when releasing captive-bred animals back into the wild, especially for apes such as orang-utans. Young apes learn from their parents about how to find food and avoid danger. If they are brought up in captivity they may need to be taught by people how to become wild again.

Future help

▼ Whale-watching not only helps people to appreciate the wonders of these great animals, but also how important it is to save all natural places and their wildlife.

373 Saving threatened animals is not just for wildlife organizations and governments — everyone can help. You could volunteer for a conservation group, or set up a wildlife club in your school or neighbourhood. You might raise awareness by telling family and friends about threatened species, or have a 'rare animals' birthday party.

374 Local zoos and wildlife parks often have lots of information about endangered animals and their conservation. You can visit, write or email them, to ask if they are involved in conservation. Find out how zoos share information about their rare animals, so suitable individuals can be brought together for breeding. Wildlife conservation organizations often offer animal adoptions so you can sponsor a rare animal, maybe as a birthday present or a gift.

375 Saving threatened animals cannot be done without saving their habitats — and taking people into account. The people who live in the same area as a rare species may be very poor and very hungry. They see lots of time and money being spent on the endangered animal, but nothing for themselves.

376 Countries and governments must take into account their people, animals, plants and habitats, for a long-term and sustainable result. For example, wildlife can help to raise money by encouraging environmentally responsible tourism. This is when people pay to see rare creatures, such as gorillas, whales and tigers, under careful, monitored conditions. Then the money is used for local conservation that helps people as well as wildlife. Only in this way can people and endangered animals live together for the future.

I DON'T BELIEVE IT!

In 2005, a new kind of monkey, the highland mangabey, was discovered in Africa. At the same time it became one of the rarest and most threatened of all animal species.

▶ A close-up view of a tiger can encourage tourists to support campaigns to save these beautiful animals, and thereby protect large areas of their habitat for other creatures and plants.

Index

Entries in **bold** refer to main subject entries. Entries in *italics* refer to illustrations

A

African hunting dog 27, *27*
agamid lizards 101
agouti 135
albatrosses 49, *49*, 67
alligator snapping turtle 117, *117*
alligators 86, 122, *122*
amphibians,
 babies **92–93**
 displays 100
 flying **106–107**
 threatened **125**
amphisbaenians 86, *86*
Andean condor 49, *49*
anole lizards 100, *100*
antbirds 79, *79*
antelopes 43, 129
Arctic tern 60, *60*
armadillos 28, *28*
arrow-poison frogs 117
auks 46, 129
axolotl 93, *93*
aye-aye 20, *20*

B

badgers 41, *41*
bald eagle 58, *58*
basilisks 110, *111*
bats 11, *11*, 16, *16*, 17, 21, 32, *32*, 38, *38*
beaks (bills) 46, 47, 68, **82–83**
bears 27, 43, *43*
bee hummingbird 48, *48*, 67, *67*
beluga sturgeon 145, *145*
biodiversity 138
birds,
 colonies *64*
 eggs **66–67**
 flightless **74–75**
 hunters **68–69**
 migration **60–61**, 145
 nests **58–59**
 nocturnal **56–57**
 parental care **70–71**
 river **76–77**
 threatened *142*, 145
birds of paradise 55, *55*, 72
bison *43*, 152, *152*
black mamba snake 111
black-necked crane 141, *141*
blue-collared lizards *86*
blue-tongued skink 121, *121*

blue whale 10, *10*, 151
bonobo 23, *23*
Born Free Foundation *150*
bowerbirds 54, *54*
Brazilian gold frog 97
burrowing mammals **40–41**
bustard 48

C

cactus wren 63, *63*
caecilians 86, *87*, 109
caimans *86*
camels 24, 25, *25*
captive breeding **154–155**
capybara 11, *11*
Caspian seals 142
cassowaries 75
cave swiftlet 59
chaffinch *46*, 71
chameleons 97, *99*, *99*, 104, *104*, 119
cheetah 12, *12*
Chelonians *115*
chevrotain 11
Chinese salamander *97*, 143
CITES 147
climate change 125, **144–145**
cobras *100*
cock-of-the-rock 55, *55*
cockatoos *46*
cold-blooded animals 84
colugo 17
conservation 133, 136, 150, 156
constricting snakes 116
courser 63
croaker fish 142
crocodiles 86, *86*, 96, **97**, *97*, 98, 122, *122*
 eggs 94
 hunting 105, *105*
crossbill 82, *82*
cuckoo 59

D

Darwin, Charles 148
deer 11, *11*, 155, *155*
desert horned lizard 120, *120*
Devil's Hole pupfish 137, *137*
dinosaurs 122
dipper 77
dodo 129, *129*
dolphins 15, 37, 143, *143*
ducks 51, 71
dugongs 39

E

echidna 8, *8*

echolocation 21, 37, 56
egg-laying mammals 8
eggs,
 amphibians 92, *93*
 birds 47, *47*, **66–67**
 reptiles 94, *94*, 123
eider duck 47, 51, *51*
elephants *8*, 10, 36, 131, *131*, 146
emperor penguin 66, 70, *70*
emu 74, *74*
endangered animals 124–125, **126–157**
ermine 18
evolution 148
extinction 124, **128–129**, 133, 149

F

falconets 49, *49*
falcons 50, *50*, 70, *70*
feathers 44, 46, *46*, 54, 55, *56*
ferrets 155
finches 148, *148*
fire-bellied toad 119, *119*
fire salamander 93, 117, *117*
flamingos 82, 83, *83*
flightless birds **74–75**
flying amphibians **106–107**
flying lemurs 17, *17*
flying reptiles **106–107**
flying squirrels 17
food chains 26, *38*
foxes 24, *24*, 34, *34*
frilled lizard 101, *101*
frog spawn 92, 93
frogs *85*, 86, *87*, 90, 113, 117, *117*, *118*
 calling 101, *101*
 moulting 108
 tadpoles 92
fur (hair) 6, 18, *18*, 24, 25, 31, 37
fur trade 151

G

gannets 53, *53*
geckos 97, 98, *98*, 103, *103*, 106, *119*
geese 51, 60, **60–61**, 71
gerbils 24, *24*
gharial *86*
giant anteater 33, *33*
giant panda 32, *32*, 43, 141, 150, *150*, 154
giant salamanders 143

giant tortoises 110, *110*, 114, 125, 148, *148*
gila monsters 120, *120*
giraffe 11, *11*
global warming 144, 145
golden eagle 68, *69*
gorillas 6, 11, *11*, *130*, 134, *134*
grass snakes 113
Great Barrier Reef 152, *152*
great crested newt *100*
grebes 55
green turtles *113*, 115, 124, *124*
greenhouse gases 144
ground squirrel 19, *19*
guillemots 64, *64*
gulls 46

H

habitat loss 134, 135, **138–141**, 149, 152
Hamilton's frog 137, *137*
hares 12, *12*, 18
harpy eagle 73, *73*
Hawaiian crow 133, *133*
hawks 70
hedgehogs 25
herons 77
hibernation 19, 86, 91, *91*
hippopotamus 36, *37*
hoatzin 73, *73*
honeyguides 78
hornbills 58, *58*
howler monkeys 30, *30*
hummingbirds 44, 46, 48, *48*, 50, *50*, 67, *67*, 79, *79*
hyenas 21, *21*

I

iguanas 103, *103*, 111, *112*, 155, *155*
IUCN 132

J

jacana 77, *77*
jaguar 30, *30*, 126
Japanese salamander 97, 143
junglefowl 72

K

kakapo 57, *57*
kangaroo 9, 9, 13, *13*
kangaroo rat 25
killer whale 15, *15*
kingfishers 76, *76*
kiwi 57, *57*, 67, 75
koala 33
Komodo dragons 122, 123, *123*

L

leafy sea dragon *132*
leatherback turtle *94*
lemmings 9
lemurs 149, *149*
leopard frog *104*
lilytrotter 77
lions 23, *26*, *130*
lizards 86, *86*, 111, 119, 120, *120*, 121, *121*, 122, *122*
    eggs 94
    flying *106*
Lonesome George 125
lorikeets *46*

M

mallard *71*
malleefowl 59
mammals,
    babies **42–43**
    burrows **40–41**
    mothers **42–43**
    nocturnal **20–21**
    plant-eaters **38–39**
mammary glands 8
manatees 39, *39*
mangabeys 157
meerkat 22, *22*
metamorphosis 92
mice 35, *35*
migration 60, 115, 145
moles 41, *41*
monitor lizards 101, 122
monk seal 129, 141, *141*
monkeys 31, 39, *139*
monotremes 8
moulting 108, *108*
musk ox 19, *19*

N

naked mole rat 23
newts 86, *87*, *91*, *100*, 113, *113*
    tadpoles 92
    tails 99
nightingale 54
nocturnal birds **56–57**
nocturnal mammals **20–21**
nocturnal reptiles 88, *103*
northern fur seal 132, *132*

O

opossums 42
orangutans 155
ospreys 76, *76*
ostrich 44, 48, *48*, 67, *67*, 74
otters 36, **37**
owls 56, *56*, 62, *62*, 80, *80*

P

Panamanian golden frogs *125*
pangolin 29, *29*
parrots *46*, 57, 72
partridges 66
partula snails 149, *149*
passenger pigeon 128
peafowl 54, *54*, 73
Pere David's deer 155, *155*
pelicans 77, *77*
penguins 52, *52*, 66, 70, *70*, *75*, 80, 144, *144*
pet trade 149
petrels 48, 136, *136*, 137
pigeons 70, 128
placental mammals 8, *8*
platypus 8, 37, *37*
plovers 61, *61*
poaching **146–147**
poison-dart frogs *117*
poisons 116, 117
polar bear 18, *18*, 144, *144*
pollution 125, **142–143**
porcupine 28
pouched mammals 8
prairie dogs 40, *40*
pronghorn 12
ptarmigan 80, *80*
pygmy marbled newt *91*
pythons 116

Q

Queen Alexandra's birdwing
    butterfly 137, *137*
quetzal 73, *73*

R

rabbits 39, 135
raccoons 35, *35*
racerunner lizards 111
rats 34, **35**
rattlesnakes 116, 121, *121*
ravens 69, *69*
Red List, IUCN 132
red panda 21, 141, *141*
reindeer 9, 18, *18*
reptiles,
    aquatic 112
    Chelonians **114–115**
    displays 100
    eggs **94–95**
    flying **106–107**
    threatened **124–125**
rhea 74, *75*, *75*
rhinoceros 29, *29*, 134, *134*, 146, *146*
right whales 135, *135*

river birds **76–77**
roadrunners 51, *75*
robins 154
rocket frogs 107
rodents 11

S

salamanders 86, *87*, *91*, *96*, 113, 117, *117*, 143
    hunting 105
    tadpoles 92, *93*
sand lizard 89
sandgrouse 62, *62*
Save the Whale 151
scarlet macaw 72, *72*
sea cow 128, *128*
sea eagle 68
sea lions 14
sea snakes 112, 113, *113*
seahorse 147, *147*
seals 14, 15, *15*, 19, 22
    endangered 129, 132, *132*, 141, *141*, 142
sheathbills 81, *81*
shingleback lizard 121, *121*
sidewinder *108*
skimmer 82
skunks 28, *28*
sloths 31, *31*
slow worms 95, *95*
smooth newt 99
snail kite 82, *82*
snakes 86, *86*, 111, 113, 116, 119, *119*
    eggs 94, *95*
    flying *106*
    hunting 105
    organs *109*
    senses 102, *102*
    skin 108, *108*, 109, *109*
snow bunting 81
snow leopard 133, *133*
spadefoot toad 89, *89*
spider monkey 139
Steller's sea cow 128, *128*
stoats 18
stoop *50*
Surinam toad 93
swallows 145
swans 71, *71*, 81, *81*
swifts *46*, 51, *51*

T

tadpoles 92, *92*
tapirs 31, *31*
tawny frogmouth 65, *65*
terrapins 114, 136

thorny devil *88*
thylacine 129, *129*
tigers 26, *26*, 147, 151, *155*, *157*
toads 86, *87*, *90*, 92, *93*, 113, 118, 119
tortoises 86, *86*, **114–115**, 148, *148*
    eggs 94
    shells 98
    speed 110
toucans *46*, 83, *83*
tourism 141, 157, *157*
tree frogs *97*, *101*, 107
tree skink 120
tuatara 86, *86*, 111, *111*
turtles 86, *86*, 94, 98, 113, *113*, **114–115**, 117, 124, 136

V

vipers *116*
vultures 49, 62, 63, *63*

W

waders *46*
Wallace's flying frog *107*
walrus 19
warm-blooded animals 6
water dragons 110
water vole 36, *36*
weaver bird 45, 59, *59*
whale conservation 150
whale-watching 156
whales 14, *14*, 15, *15*, 22, 33, *33*, 42, *42*, 135, *135*
wildebeest 27
wings,
    bats 16, *16*
    birds 44, 46, *46*, 49, 50, *50*, 56
wolves 22, *22*
wombat 135
woodpecker *46*, 67, *67*, 78, *78*
World Heritage Sites 153
World Wildlife Fund 150
wrybill 83, *83*

Z

zebra 26, 38, *38*

Acknowledgements

The publishers would like to thank the following sources for the use of their photographs:
Key: t = top, b = bottom, l = left, r = right, c = centre, bg = background

Front cover illustration Stuart Jackson Carter **Spine** Visuals Unlimited/Nature Picture Library **Back cover** (clockwise from l) Incredible Arctic/Shutterstock, Eduardo Rivero/Shutterstock, LeonP/Shutterstock, Anton_Ivanov/Shutterstock, Joe Farah/Shutterstock

Alamy 79(tr) David Tipling; 144–145(tc) WorldFoto

Ardea 96(tr) Ken Lucas

Born Free 150(tr) www.bornfree.org.uk

Dreamstime 49(tc) Chmelars; 65(tl) Thesmid; 75(cr) Lukyslukys; 82(bl) Steve Byland

FLPA 13(t) Theo Allofs/Minden Pictures; 15(b) Norbert Wu/Minden Pictures; 24(tr) Imagebroker/Konrad Wothe; 25(b) ImageBroker; 31(br) Mark Newman; 35(b) Michael Durham/Minden Pictures; 41(c) John Eveson; 48(bl) Kevin Elsby; 51(bl) Roger Tidman; 54(bl) & 152–153(tc) David Hosking; 57(br) ImageBroker; 68–69(c) Imagebroker/Horst Jegen; 70(bl) ImageBroker; 72(c) Jurgen & Christine Sohns; 73(tr) Konrad Wothe/Minden Pictures; 77(br) Shem Compion; 81(cr) Imagebroker/Dieter Hopf; 87(table br) Michael & Patricia Fogden/Minden Pictures; 88–89(bg) Fred Bavendam/Minden Pictures; 91(bl) Emanuele Biggi; 93(t) Bruno Cavignaux/Biosphoto; 112(c) Tui De Roy/Minden Pictures; 114–115(c) Pete Oxford/Minden Pictures; 119(c) Piotr Naskrecki/Minden Pictures; 122–123(c) Cyril Ruoso/Minden Pictures; 124–125(c) Nicolas-Alain Petit/Biosphoto; 125(tl) Imagebroker/Ingo Schulz; 126–127(c) Frans Lanting; 132(bl) Winfried Wisniewski; 151(c) Flip Nicklin/Minden Pictures; 154(b) Katherine Feng/Globio/Minden Pictures;

Fotolia.com 75(bg) pdtnc; 86(table tr) Becky Stares; 86(table cl) reb; 86(table bl) Eric Gevaert; 86(table br) SLDigi; 88(panel tr) Alexey Khromushin; 91(c) Shane Kennedy; 99(panel cl) Konstantin Sutyagin; 115(panel tr) Irochka

Getty 33(br) Tom Brakefield; 40(c) Dorling Kindersley; 52–53(c) Paul Souders; 52–53(cl) Kevin Schafer; 74(tr) John Carnemolla; 81(cr) Rick Price; 104(t) Gary Meszaros; 116(bl) David A. Northcott; 130(b) Martin Harvey; 131(c) Art Wolfe; 140(c) Fernando Bengoechea; 142(tr) Karen Kasmauski; 143(bl) George Steinmetz; 143(br) Mark Carwardine; 147(r) Owen Franken; 153(tr) Martin Harvey; 157(br) Theo Allofs; 138–139(c) Mint Images/Frans Lanting; 152–153(bc) Theo Allofs; 155(tl) National Geographic; 156–157(c) Natalie Fobes

Glow Images 14(c) Superstock; 23(b) Terry Whittaker; 34 Juniors Bildarchive; 38(cl) Rolf Nussbaumer

International Reptile Conservation Foundation 155(cr) John F. Binns/www.IRCF.org

iStockphoto.com 144(b) Coldimages; 60–61(bg) ElsvanderGun

National Geographic Creative 10(l) Hiroya Minakuchi/Minden Pictures; 17(c) & 55(cl) Tim Laman; 31(b) Nicole Duplaix; 58(bl) Klaus Nigge; 148(br) Pete Oxford/Minden Pictures

Nature Picture Library 6–7(c) T.J. Rich; 27(t) Andy Rouse; 27(b) & 29(r) Jabruson; 32(tr) Jim Clare; 57(tr) Mark Carwardine; 76(tl) Rolf Nussbaumer; 83(cr) Andrew Walmsley; 94(t) Jurgen Freund; 95(b) Laurie Campbell; 99(br) Russell Cooper; 101(c) Dave Watts; 106(c) Tim MacMillan/John Downer Pro; 107(t) Stephen Dalton; 110–111(c) Bence Mate; 114(cl) Michael Richards/John Downer; 120(bl) John Cancalosi; 125(br) Visuals Unlimited; 141(tr) Wild Wonders of Europe/SÃ¡

Photoshot 21(c) Imago; 90(bl) NHPA; 108(c) NHPA; 117(tr) NHPA; 130(c) & 146–147(c) Jonathan & Angela Scott/NHPA

Save The Rhino 134(tr) Save the Rhino International

Shutterstock.com 1 infografick; 2–3 Johan Larson; 4–5(t) Darryl Vest; 8(t) Norma Cornes; 9(t) BMJ; 9(bl), (b) & 18(c) Incredible Arctic; 9(t) Smileus; 11(b) Chainfoto24; 12(bl) Neil Burton; 12(c) Mark Beckwith; 14–15(c) jaytee; 16–17(c) Sarun T; 18(b) Magdanatka; 19(b) Zoltan Katona; 22(bl) EcoPrint; 22(tr) outdoorsman; 24–25(bg) Bozena Fulawka; 26(b) Mogens Trolle; 28(bl) Ultrashock; 30(tr) & 47(bc) BMJ; 30–31(bg) theerapol sri–in; 31(tl) & 54–55(tc) & 75(tr) & 84–85(c) & 119(cr) Eric Isselee; 35(tr) trancedrumer; 36–37(bg) Anna Om; 37(tr) & 73(bl, br) & 105(c) worldswildlifewonders; 38(b) EcoPrint; 39(br) Andrea Izzotti; 43(br) Jean-Edouard Rozey; 44–45(c) Atul Sinai Borker; 46(bc) nuttakit; 46(tr) Grant Glendinning; 46(cl) Florian Andronache; 46(c) Eduardo Rivero; 46(cr) Clinton Moffat; 48(bl) monbibi; 48(c) Sergei25; 50(bl) ktsdesign; 51(tr) AndreAnita; 53(tr) WayneDuguay; 56(c) Alfredo Maiquez; 60(tr) Gregg Williams; 60(c) Arto Hakola; 60–61(t, bl, c) Johan Swanepoel; 60–61(tc, b) & 72(tl) monbibi; 63(t) T.Allendorf; 63(tr) tntphototravis; 63(bc) Stu Porter; 64(c) Jerome Whittingham; 65(br) Kimberley McClard; 67(tc) picturepartners; 67(br) IbajaUsap; 69(br) David Dohnal; 70(tr) Gentoo Multimedia Limited; 71(b) Karel Gallas; 71(tc) Jan de Wild; 74–75(c) John Carnemolla; 75(tr) Anton_Ivanov; 75(tr) & 87(table bl) Jason Mintzer; 76(bl) Richard Fitzer; 77(tl)zimmytws; 78(cl) FloridaStock; 80–81(c) Rob McKay; 83(tr) fotofactory; 85(tr) Anneka; 86(b) Joe Farah; 87(tr) Mircea Bezergheanu; 87(table t) Dirk Ercken; 87(table cl) Brandon Alms; 87(table cr) Salim October; 89(tr) iliuta goean; 90(b) monbibi; 90–91(c) Brian Lasenby; 93(bl) AdStock RF; 95(panel tr) Asaf Eliason; 96–97(c) Meister Photos; 97(br) Brandon Alms; 97(br) Eduard Kyslynskyy; 99(tr) infografick; 100(br) Manja; 101(tl) clearviewstock; 102(b) Statsenko; 102–103(c) Ivan Kuzmin; 103(bl) Anneka; 104(b) Cathy Keifer; 106(panel b) Madlen; 106–107(bg) Iakov Kalinin; 106(panel b) J. L. Levy; 113(bg) Rich Carey; 118(c) alslutsky; 121(b) Audrey Snider-Bell; 133(tr) Dennis W Donohue; 142(bl) wim claes;

Superstock 55(br) Biosphoto

All other photographs are from: DigitalSTOCK, digitalvision, John Foxx, PhotoAlto, PhotoDisc, PhotoEssentials, PhotoPro, Stockbyte

All artworks are from the Miles Kelly Artwork Bank

Every effort has been made to acknowledge the source and copyright holder of each picture.
Miles Kelly Publishing apologizes for any unintentional errors or omissions.